NO MORE Ms Nice Girl

A guide in learning to say "Yes" to yourself

Toni Dowrey

This book is dedicated to all the women who have been giving and pleasing others and are now willing to say YES to themselves. You deserve it!

Introduction

If you continue giving others all your food, you will eventually starve. Caring enough to share is an excellent quality you should have, but depleting yourself for the sake of others is death. It would be best if you fed yourself first. It is like when the air flight attendant gives life-saving instructions and states that you must put on your own oxygen mask before helping others. In life, you must give to yourself before giving to others. It is hard to stop that behavior if you are a giver, pleaser, and peacemaker. You give, you please, and you try so hard to make others happy, but at what expense to yourself? Do you get depleted and exhausted physically and/or mentally from giving too much of yourself? Because you weren't designed to do this over and over and over. It is time to stop!

This book will guide you in changing your behavior, allowing you to say yes to yourself and know when to say yes to others. You will learn how to clear your thoughts and shed your 'nice girl' ways to move on to a better life for yourself. Also, you will learn to be confident when you say yes to what is important to your life and know there is no guilt or shame in making yourself happy. Being a nice person is excellent! However, being a nice girl can be your enemy, as it can deplete your life.

This book took ten years to write because I needed to be in a place where my advice came from a trusted source. Me! It took me *too many years* of being the *nice girl* to figure this out. But after much self-neglect and pleasing others, I am free to be myself, do what is good for me, and do what I want and need. Do I consider others? Of course, but I do what is best for me first. Leaving the *nice girl's* ways and changing my direction has been the best action of my life.

I hope that others will not wait as long. If you feel drained from always giving yourself to others and not yourself, only you can change that. Don't wait! Take control over your own life and live on your own terms. Be kind, be nice, be giving—just don't be the *Nice Girl!*

Chapters

Chapter One

The Nice Girl

Being the nice girl can get you far...... but not being the
nice girl can get you further ~TD

The definition of nice... *pleasant in manner, good-natured, kind.* Nice people are great to hang around. It is even better to be a nice person. But what about being *too* nice? Well, you can be, and most of the time, it's those *nice girls. Nice girls* are everywhere! They come in all ages, shapes, and colors. They can be in any city, suburb, or rural county. A *nice girl* can even be you!

Nice girls are more than being sweet and wishing someone a great day. Many nice people are like this, but wouldn't you rather want to leave a glow wherever you go? Want people to say positive things about you? Want others to feel great in your presence? Not stir up problems, but rather leave a good impression on everyone you come in contact with? Most *nice girls* do. Some just want to be nice and expect everyone else to be this way, too. But many *nice girls* want to leave a stupendous wake behind them, full of niceness that others can ride on like a wave. There is nothing wrong with being nice. The world definitely can use more nice people, but being the *nice girl* needs to stop.

A nice person is not the same as a *nice girl*. A nice person is friendly and considerate, bringing a pleasant atmosphere with them. Many people are nice and carry a positive vibe, which is why others like to keep them around to feel good. A *nice girl,* on the other hand, is someone who sacrifices so that others can have. A *nice girl* gives to others and expects nothing in return (but would like it). A *nice girl* tries to please everyone and makes sure things are peaceful. A *nice girl* will say yes to everyone so their feelings don't get hurt, even if hers will. A *nice girl* dreams of a life where she hopes that one day *her* dreams will come true, but in reality, she continues to help others fulfill their dreams first. A *nice girl* will fill her calendar to tiresome standards to please everyone, even if she struggles to keep up. A *nice girl* will do whatever she needs to lift others, even if it leaves her feeling let down.

If you are reading this book, *you may* be a *nice girl,* and enough is enough. It is time to move on from these behaviors and leave some of this niceness behind. Everyone has their limits, and your limit is here. And it is okay. It is okay to let go. It is okay to move on. It is okay to say that it is just enough. It is okay not to be the nice girl anymore.

This book does refer to the *nice girl,* but, of course, you can be the nice *guy,* too. People tend to think of men as strong, tough, and slightly badass, but many are very sweet and kind and have the same problems as the *nice girl.* They are always looking out for others instead of looking out for themselves. Men also try to please and use their energy for others instead of focusing on what they want or need. So even though this book refers to the nice *girl,* this can also be translated to the nice *guy.*

Many people like *nice girls.* They are so good to have around to get everyone's needs handled. The problem with you being the *nice girl* is that, eventually, you will get tired. Tired of being so busy. Tired of always wanting to please. Tired of the emotional energy it takes to keep peace. Tired of the physical strain of trying to keep up. Tired of not taking care of yourself. Tired of being just plain tired! After a while, it wears on you.

You may not even mentally notice it, but your body will. You may start to feel run down. You may feel the leap in your skip is less than a step. You may feel your emotions start to dull. It can be exhausting. You know something is off. You know something just isn't right. You know something needs to change.

Being a *nice girl* can make you feel less of yourself. Everyone else is being boosted and lifted except you. You give so much of yourself to others that you don't have enough reserve to boost and lift yourself. Some of the nicest people who dedicate much of themselves often feel empty. They struggle to find something they feel is missing. They are so busy helping others fill the voids in their lives that their own voids never get filled. The cycle of constantly giving can also become constantly draining. They continually pour it out to others without others giving any of it back.

Can you relate to some of this? Are you the one who volunteers for everything? Do you put others' needs before your own regularly? Do you feel drained from giving so much of yourself to others that you don't have anything left to give yourself?

It is not wrong to help others, but it is detrimental when you neglect to help yourself. Being nice makes you a wonderful person, but even nice *people* have limits. You may be a *nice girl* when you give way more of yourself to the outside world and don't replenish yourself on the inside. You will eventually have nothing more to offer if you don't get some balance in your life and change your ways.

So why do you insist on helping others before yourself? Why are you always being so nice? Why are you always trying to keep the peace and not stand up for yourself? Why are you always handing it out to others but not allowing yourself to receive it? Why do you just plain keep giving in? It could be a few different reasons. Let's look at some possibilities.

Some *nice girls* could just be born this way. It is in their DNA. They really cannot help it. It is part of their genetic traits from simply being who they are when they are born. But do not use 'you were born this way' as an excuse because you most likely were not. But it may feel that way because, starting at a young age, people have been raised to behave in specific ways, especially females. They are taught to be polite, have manners, not upset others, don't cause a scene, and be nice to everybody. This is not bad. Don't most people want to be good and nice to others? This teaches you to be a classy lady and present yourself well. The problem with this is that it has hurt far too many young ladies and, in many situations, continued into late adulthood. They were raised to be nice, way too nice, and with no boundaries being set. There is no control over this niceness, and these girls are taught to be too nice to everyone, regardless of how they are treated.

This is no fault of the *nice girl*. When you are taught something, especially by a parent, family member, or authority figure, you just assume it is right and do as you are told (or taught) as a child. When you are trained to act a certain way for many years, it just gets instilled in you. And when the word *you* is being used in this book, it is a general you, not *you* directly. Unless it just happens to apply, it would be *you*. Anyway, a taught behavior is the most common.

Of course, you want to be polite and not rude; you don't want to hurt anybody's feelings or be disrespectful. And self-control is an important quality to have while not making a scene or completely freaking out on someone. You need to learn the limits. How far do you go in being nice and respectful? What is the limit, and how do you stop when you have given enough or way too much? How do you control your emotions until you can't take it anymore? Many people who are taught these 'being nice' standards as children are now learning to put themselves as a first priority and give back to themselves, as they are now depleted and wish they had learned sooner to change this behavior. There are women in their fifties and beyond who are struggling with what they have been taught and want to be in more control of their own lives. They are finding it very difficult after many years of this being embedded into their heads, and still being taught no differently, the older they get.

Since the day these *nice girls* could remember, they were told to act in specific ways, which allowed them to be liked, loved, and accepted. For generations, it has always been pushed to help and put others before yourself. They are taught to share their things, meaning nothing is really theirs. They are told to get along well with others and respect their elders, people of authority, and society. Do not upset anyone and do as you are told. You can't just go around showing off your emotions and you need to suck up your feelings while trying please others. So, it is taught from a young age how to behave and be '*nice.*'

Being raised as a *nice girl* makes it difficult for her to prioritize her own well-being, and she will not take charge of her own needs. She has been taught that putting yourself first is not proper behavior; it is selfish and not allowed. But there is no gratification in the long run for being too nice. Initially, she will happily help others and do things for them, perhaps even to the point of finding it gratifying. Then, it will become a burden that she cannot stop, and she will continue because she feels she has to, in her mind's eye. Eventually, she will become depleted and resentful.

In some situations, she may not have been raised this way through verbal instruction, but rather by observation. She may have seen her mom put all her efforts into others and feels that she needs to be the same way to have respect or acceptance from her mom or other people around her. She must meet or exceed what she was raised with. Many children act in accordance with the environment in which they are raised. If her mom was involved in the PTA, hosting parties, helping with work meetings, and had a full calendar, a young girl may feel she needs to be this way as an adult, too. It is either a way of life or a way of acceptance. She may follow a pattern that wasn't hers but is now struggling to escape it.

As people live, they become molded by life. Experience and emotions can affect how you act and respond toward others. Some may be molded into pleasers. Life has hit them in a place where they feel the only way to survive in life is by making others happy. People pleasers tend to be the nicest and most helpful people you know. They never say no when asked to do something; you can always count on them. They can be the first to volunteer; even if they aren't, they will do it if asked. People are amazed by how much this person can get done. They admire the pleaser and wish they were as nice and helpful. Many wish they had the energy to do all those things they do. The pleaser sets a standard that others want to follow or become. But they also get taken for granted, and people use them for their own benefit. All the while, this *nice girl* is in a very unhealthy behavioral pattern and striving towards an endless goal.

This *nice girl* is an overachiever when it comes to helping others. She will complete her tasks and assist others with theirs as well. She will drive everyone around as a taxi, fix countless meals for the needy, help with event activities, plan and coordinate work functions, meet deadlines, and go beyond expectations to please everyone along the way. Still, she will not find time to relax and work on her own needs. She will be busy all day until it is time for bed, and even then, she will have late nights. While to others, she seems to be the most helpful, well-organized, and put-together person, the fact is, she is often acting this way out of fear of failure or rejection. Her pleasing will continue to escalate as she searches for feelings of worth and appreciation.

This *nice girl* may have been rejected at some point. She may have been bullied in school, criticized by parents or friends, or possibly been in an abusive relationship, or some other event that has led to a need to please. Sometimes, it can be from a family or relationship environment that had been or is emotionally unattached, and she is finding outside sources to fill this void. She will work diligently to please everyone except herself. This may be an unconscious behavior. She may not even realize why she is doing this and what she is trying to accomplish. She is fighting a battle she cannot win until she discovers that the only person she needs to please and be focused on *is* herself. She will constantly try to find the worthiness she seeks, but will never achieve accurate fulfillment.

Some *nice girls* harbor everything inside and just let the nice play out. It isn't about anyone else but rather about her piece of mind. She plays along and keeps everyone happy as a way to get along through life with little complication. She doesn't always agree with others, but she doesn't disagree either. She won't discuss much of herself to avoid judgment. She will hold back opinions and emotions so she will not disappoint. She is pleasing to others in their presence, but doesn't feel the same alone. She is putting on a front; she isn't being true to herself. She is also not being true to others. She lets it ride to get through another day, trying to avoid any actual conflict or emotional concern, almost to the point of feeling numb. She is not serving herself in any way but avoidance.

She may not like confrontation—most nice girls don't—or she may have been put down for her opinions or feelings in a way that has left a lasting negative impact. She feels she should keep her honest opinions and feelings to herself, allowing others to think she is the nicest person to be around. And she is. She is just not being true to herself, others, or the life she wishes to live. She will continue to become numb to herself and her actual being.

It could also be that a *nice girl* may be in a bad situation. She could be emotionally bruised. It could be work, family, lover, or friends. She could be in a situation where someone else needs control, so she goes along with everything to keep things calm and non-abusive. Abuse is not always physical. Any abuse can lead someone to close up and be "nice" and compliant as a way to survive. She may feel that her feelings are not valid. That her thoughts or opinions do not matter. Her true self is not allowed to be expressed. So, she hides who she is to keep peace in her environment. She does not discuss this with others and hides it to be safe. The outside world sees her as quiet and calm. She's such a pleasure to be around. Inside, she is trying to survive and not cause harm to herself by losing a job, relationship, or being attacked physically, verbally, or emotionally. But once she opens out of this 'safe' box she has formed around her, finds her truth, and starts to reveal it, her world will be better for it, and she will thrive.

There is a pattern. Most *nice girls* are seeking acceptance, but some need it more. They will seek compliments, reassurance, friendships, and positive feedback. They may be lacking self-confidence or acceptance in their life. These *nice girls* will find outside sources to get the acceptance or attention they need. They will be on boards or committees, serve as organization leaders, volunteer for their kids' activities, be school moms, or push harder than others at work. They are continually filling a void they desire to fill. And it will get filled now and then, but not enough. So, it will just continue.

Constantly seeking compliments or positive feedback is exhausting mentally and physically. Her primary goal in being nice and helping others is to feel needed and for somebody to continue to want her. She may realize what she is doing and be okay with this. She wants to feel like she belongs and has meaning. The girl who seeks so much from the outside is the one who must indeed find it from the inside. Everyone wants some acceptance, especially from the ones they love. However, this girl is searching for something to be satisfied with. She will continue to push harder to find it, even to the point of almost being broken. What she needs to find is her inner peace. When she does, she will find that all her hard work has genuinely helped her see what she has had all along.

The previously listed *nice girls* need to change. Although they mostly hurt themselves, they can also be problematic for others. But the one hurting themselves and others most often is not the *nice girl* who cares and does so much for others, but rather the one who enables. Especially those who have made poor choices and have bad behavior. She has difficulty saying no to her friends, children, spouse, parents, or other family and friends. She allows their behavior because she does not want to let anyone down. She wants to be there for them. Care for them. Be their savior. But they are either using her for something or draining her emotional energy. The *nice girl* does not want to see others hurt or suffer, so she is there to assist them, regardless of what it does to her well-being or how it hinders the others from caring for themselves and learning life responsibilities. This will continue until the people no longer need her and move on, leaving her feeling empty and hurt for all the time and care she put into them without a 'thank you' for all she did.

This *nice girl* often stays up for hours worrying, talking, advising, or listening to them vent. Over and over and over again. They drain her emotionally and physically with their pity me or drama stories. They are harmful, hurtful, pitiful, or angry at the world. She lets them go on even though they take so much of her time, keeping her from doing what she wants or needs to do. She can't say no to avoid disappointing them or hurting their feelings.

She also enables others not to be independent, functional, and productive people. She will allow her children to do everything they want so they are happy. She will keep her children in their homes long after graduation to avoid them struggling independently. She will cater to the family's needs, so they don't have to do it themselves. She will be run down but will not ask for help, and no one will offer. She will do it for everyone, but not for herself.

This hurts the *nice girl* physically and emotionally. She feels like a servant instead of a wife, mom, or friend. She feels like the glue holding everything together and can't break that seal. It can be overwhelming, but she still allows it to continue. She is so fixated on keeping peace and making everyone happy that she doesn't realize the damage it causes others. They are not learning to help themselves, do not understand the value of others, and do not respect the efforts and time given to them. They will take and take, and this behavior will not stop until the *nice girl* decides to change. When she does, she will be healing herself while helping others. The others will not see it as helpful to them, and this is where battles can occur, but it must be done. If the *nice girl* won't do it for herself, she must do it for them. She will also benefit and reap much by letting others do for themselves.

Do you relate to any of this? Some may ask, *What is wrong with being a nice person? Why would you want or need to change?* Absolutely nothing is wrong with being a nice person. We should all be nice people, but there are differences. A nice person is someone pleasant to be around. You appreciate their company; they can be reliable and caring. The *nice girl* makes unhealthy choices to please others instead of pleasing or taking care of herself. If you are reading this book, you may be a *nice girl* and know exactly what this is about. You are at the point where you just can't or don't want to be this way anymore. You deserve more from your life, including yourself, and you are one step closer to that happening. Good work for taking this time for you!

Your body is designed to heal itself. It replenishes so you can keep going. There are limits on how far you want to push yourself. You cannot keep neglecting yourself for the sake of others. Instead of taking time to be healthy and prioritizing self-care, are you just fragments of what you want to be? Eventually, you will realize you are not giving your entire self to others. You are giving what pieces you can find because you are so scattered and possibly even shattered to provide much more. When you finally start putting yourself first and replenishing, you will have more of your true self to offer.

Helping others is fulfilling. Being a secretary on the PTA is terrific. Being a Cub Mom or Girl Scout Leader is fabulous. Being the taxi driver, your job's special committee member, or the baseball scorekeeper is fantastic. These duties can bring fulfillment as long as you take time for yourself. It is about balance. You cannot weigh yourself down with tasks for others and not balance that with taking care of yourself. Self-neglect is the most significant side effect of being a *nice girl*. After a while, your body will feel it and suffer from it. It can take a heavy toll. You do not want all of your nice gestures to end up as a hurtful memory because you became broken or sick.

The *nice girl* also tends to feel a lot of stress. Now, you all know that stress can cause bodily damage. It is related to many health issues. When you are a nice girl, you stress about getting things done, being efficient, being recognized, being accountable, being a role model, but most of all, not letting others down. That is a lot to live up to. That can cause anyone a lot of stress. On top of just being busy, you also have your daily life to live. This can become very overwhelming.

When you are in a situation of being busy and stressed, this can also bring on depression. You may feel like you are not living up to the standards of others or yourself. It is not only the expectations of the job or task duties you are performing, but also the personal expectations that can cause the most stress and anxiety. It is the pleasing that has you all under fire and stressed out. If you can't meet the demands, you get upset with yourself, feeling like you are disappointing others, which makes you even more upset. You can start to feel very negative about your actions and abilities. You then seek that pleasing fulfillment again, which can turn into a vicious cycle.

Many times, the *nice girl* quality turns into a less enthusiastic person. There is so much to get done that there is no time to waste watching television, or family time becomes scarce because you are too busy helping others. The baseball games are not much fun to watch anymore because you're too busy keeping score or planning the next function. The Cub Mom job isn't about the good times with the cubs and your child, because it has turned into planning events and scheduling meetings. When your joy leaves the heart from the task you set out to enjoy due to being too busy or mind occupied, it is time to quit. The events that you do should be about the thrill of doing it. The fulfillment you get from the participation. If you are losing these feelings, others will notice. Often, this will bring on poor feelings from yourself or those around you.

You also have the people who will take your niceness for granted. They will use you to fulfill *their* needs, but not consider yours. You are overwhelmed, but you continue to carry these burdens not to disappoint others. Sometimes, you may take on these tasks to keep the peace. You don't complain and keep quiet to avoid a negative outcome; inside, it is tearing you up.

In more severe cases, being the *nice girl* to avoid mental or physical abuse is a reality to some. Doing what they can to be safe. Professional help is strongly recommended, and safety should be your first concern. If this is you, please get help immediately. This situation could lead to shutting down, suppressing emotions or communications with others, sadness, depression, or more abuse. Find a source to get you the help you need to escape this situation now!

Many of the *nice girls* discussed are possibly on the verge of anger, exhaustion, illness, self-destruction, and one conversation away from a meltdown. Something has to change, and soon! Even if your case is not listed or you don't feel it is extreme, if you want to step back from being the yes girl, this is for you, too.

Many of you already know you need to stop being the *nice girl*. You want to stop being taken advantage of. You want to start focusing on yourself. You want to start standing up for yourself more and learn to say no. This book will give you advice and steps to assist you in becoming not-so-nice and more empowered. This does not mean that you will not be a nice person. You will learn to be nice within boundaries while taking care of yourself.

No one wants to hurt anyone's feelings. You are nice, and that is not what you do. However, you want to start living more for yourself and enjoying your own life. You want to enjoy all the moments and take them in, not let your mind wander about what needs to be done next and how much time you have. You will learn to say no when you know it is in your best interest to do so. You will allow yourself to self-indulge because it has been forever since you have done this for yourself, and you know it is essential to do so. And you will not feel guilty for wanting your own life.

You will not feel guilty for making your own life your priority. You will not feel guilty or think you are being selfish, and you should stop this at any time. You will not take your nice away, but rather learn to balance it. You will be more of a value to yourself and others when you put your wants and needs first.

The *nice girl* is cheating herself out of things that can bring her happiness. She is so focused on everyone else's needs and wants that hers are dismissed or non-existent. As people get older, they realize this behavior has been a burden to their well-being. It is time to change! It can be hard to change these ways, but it *can* be done! And it needs to be done! The *nice girl* will lose out on so much of her own life because she is constantly helping others fulfill theirs. She now knows that it is time to re-train herself. She will come to understand that it is okay to say no. It is okay to take time for herself. It is okay not to please everyone. It is okay to follow her own dreams. And it is going to be so wonderful when she does!

It is time to begin your new adventures in life. A new journey awaits you. It is time for self-awareness, self-indulgence, and self-healing. It is time to open your heart and live fully, which includes taking care of yourself. It is time you put down your Wonder Woman bra and throw on a regular one instead. Just be a woman living your life to the fullest. You have taken on everything else, and now it is time to take this on for you. There is power in doing plenty, but there is better success when you focus on less.

Chapter Two

Nice Can Be Bad

People can only take advantage of you if you let them. ~TD

    While you think you are spreading positive vibes by being the pleaser, helper, and all-around great gal, you may be generating a negative effect instead. Being too nice can turn bad. You are doing so much to make everything right, only to make things wrong. How on earth can that be possible? Well, even the best intentions sometimes have adverse effects.

    Sometimes, being a *nice girl* can affect your family. You have all the best intentions because you love your kids and want to be there for them. You want to be a school mom, sit on the PTA, chaperone school activities, be a group leader, and be active in your children's lives. You want to be one of those moms who are very involved with the school activities and participate in everything you possibly can. The time spent with your children is precious, and you don't want to miss it. You want to absorb these moments and take them all in.

There can be a problem when you want to be overly active in your children's lives. When you are involved in too many things, you may spend too much time *away* from your family. You must attend meetings, have social discussions, prepare and plan for occasions, and more. You are trying to do these activities to help your family be close, but you are being taken from them instead. The whole point of being a part of your children's school and activities was to spend time with them, but in turn, it can be tearing you away. Too many activities on your plate mean more time to focus on other things besides your family.

It could also be quite the opposite. You may be so involved that you spend too much time with your family. Sometimes, your kids need to be in activities to have their own space outside of the family. If you are volunteering for everything and not letting your child have that space, that can become a problem. People like to have their own identity. If someone is always a part of what they do, they feel like they can't do anything alone. They may feel like they can't grow up independently and are always babied or chaperoned. You do not want to remove your children's feelings of independence, responsibility, and individuality. You want to be involved, but don't smother them. *Be a mother, but do not smother.* It's an easy way to remember that one.

You want to be a part of your children's growing years, but if you are too involved, they may not develop into their own person. They may grow up into what you want them to be, what they think you want them to be, or they may be afraid to spread their own wings and fly in their own way. You could be hindering your family instead of helping them.

22

This does not mean you cannot participate in the school programs or your child's activities. Just do your thing and let your child do theirs. Do not overcrowd your child or put too many activities on your plate so that your family time gets scarce. Let your kid be a kid and have others they can be around instead of it always being their mom. Let them expand.

If being the *nice girl* can have some negative responses from your family, it can also have negative ones on the outside. This can include friends, co-workers, employers, organizations, and school program volunteers. Not everyone thinks the *nice girl* is really all that nice. And even if she is nice, she can't please everyone, even though she tries. Of course, this is *not* true for everyone. Some people admire the *nice girl* and all of her capabilities. Some people appreciate the help and generosity. Most people do. That is why you do it. To get the praise for the beautiful job you are doing, but just like everyone else, you can't make everyone happy.

Some people do not trust nice people. They believe there is a motive behind their behavior. Although we have mentioned the motives in the previous chapter, those are not the motives that other people think. Some feel the person has a hidden agenda. They may feel that their intentions are not valid. They may feel that you are *kissing up*. They may think you are trying to appear better than others. They may feel that you are trying to work your way *in*. They may label you the boss's pet or a mini-me. They don't know you are trying to feed your self-worth or want to help. They will find fault with your actual intentions because they don't have the same gift as you. Sometimes, being a *nice girl* doesn't appear quite nice to others. Being so nice in some situations may not be in your best interest. It can be damaging.

Some people will look for or find fault in you or your actions, especially when they are not being seen as nice or appreciated as you are. If you are taking attention away from someone else or "showing them up," then they will not accept your niceness. Some may turn things to make *you* look bad. Jealousy can be a tricky and wicked thing. It can be vicious. You have seen it take form on television shows with movies based on actual events, real-life PTA meetings, or meetings at work. People can be mean when threatened by nice people. Here, you are trying to do good and receive a negative response.

This kind of reaction can tear you down and make you question what you're doing wrong. It can lead you to question your actions, behavior, trust, betrayal, and value. The reason you're being nice in the first place is often for approval. If you are not getting it, then you are defeating yourself. Although you are not trying to cause problems, you just may be. This can be very confusing and cause unwanted emotions such as anxiety, fear, or anger. It is by no fault of your own. It is just how people are. You will find some who don't appreciate your hard work and find it threatening instead. If you make others look bad because you are willing to help, smile, and do the job, you might make others unhappy.

Some people might find the *nice girl* to be less honest. If they ask for your opinion on the dance decorations for the school and you say, "It looks great!" they may wonder if you are being honest or just saying it to be nice. When someone wants honesty, they may not ask the *nice girl.* If you want to be valued in that respect, the *nice girl* may not cut it. Other times, you may be asked just because the other person knows you will say what they want to hear and validate their thought, but they are not seeking the truth.

Being nice also might make you a liar. You will lie to make others feel good and not cause a problem. For instance, when you were asked if the dance decorations looked good, and you said they looked great, they looked hideous, but you didn't want to hurt someone's feelings. You also didn't want to take the time to redo the work, and it was easier to lie. Inside, your gut is turning and causing you stress because you can't allow yourself to be honest. So, in turn, you did not do the person any favors by lying. That person may know it looks bad, but if you condone it, that leaves no room for improvement. Also, you are now feeling terrible inside for not being brave enough to tell the truth, and the other person may be upset that you lied because they wanted an honest opinion.

Lying is a bad habit to get into. It does you and others no justice. It might reduce some hurt, but there is still hurt when there is a lie. That includes little white lies. Even if it doesn't hurt others, it is hurting you. It has been studied and proven that people who lie, even to be nice and avoid offending others, have more stress and more physical and mental health complaints than those who don't lie. So, lying in the name of niceness can put psychological and physical pressure on you. You do not need that, along with others believing in your lack of honesty. Don't go around and start throwing truths out all over the place. That could be harmful, too. Sometimes, it may be best to keep quiet and avoid a response.

It is also found that nice people are followers. Not too many are leaders. This means the leaders will use the nice people in excess to benefit themselves. They do this knowing the nice person will not refuse and get the job done. Many employers overwork their employees in many of these situations. Of course, you do the work so you won't lose your job, and because the leader knows there won't be any complaints. The nice person is working harder than others. You may be given extra work because you are more reliable than other co-workers. You may have volunteered for things in the past and are still overloaded with job duties that others don't seem to have. It can be too much.

Then, there are possible problems with other groups or committees. You might be taking on much more than others if you are the nice girl in the group or committee, because the leader knows you will not say no. The extra work you are taking on takes the responsibilities away from others in the group or committee, but no one seems to resist this. It may also put too much pressure on you while lessening the load for others. It may make you look good, feel important, and give you value, but are you noticing the flaws with this, too?

Some people feel that nice people are weak or do not have a backbone. They think they can't stand up for anything or speak their minds. Here, again, how the impression of nice can be turned into a negative. People love nice people, but don't love nice people who wither, or don't show a sense of self-value. This, in turn, can be negative for you if you are this kind of *nice girl.* You will not gain the respect you deserve, and you will be walked on and abused to fulfill others' needs. That is why being nice is wonderful, but you must be firm when the timing calls for it.

Many *nice girls* do not stand up for themselves, letting conflicts go to avoid confrontation. This can cause emotions to bottle up inside and tear someone down a little bit at a time. Relationships are a good example of this. Some people like to find a weak, *nice girl*. It gives the other person a sense of power and control they need to feel for themselves. If the *nice girl* lets it go to avoid conflict, argument, or abuse, the other person thrives on this to build their ego. This is an abusive and toxic relationship. This kind of relationship isn't even about being the *nice girl,* but instead a traumatized girl who is just trying to survive.

Other people will find the weakness in the *nice girl,* too. If you are involved in your child's activities, you will notice some school employees or moms taking advantage of this. Some moms can be on the "not-so-nice" list. They will seek out and find those *nice girls* and use them. They will ask them to pick up their kid for practice, bring snacks, or be the scorekeeper so that they can walk around and socialize. You may not be weak, but if you are nice and say yes to them, it can be a sign of weakness, even if you want to do it for your enjoyment. Eventually, you keep saying yes so you won't cause a conflict, the sign of your weakness.

What about being boring? When you are constantly being nice and trying to please others, this can present you as passive and boring. How much fun is it if you always agree or don't make a final decision? Not much. If you always leave it up to other people and then agree with them, it gives no room for growth or going outside the box. People get bored with doing only what they want to do all the time.

They want friends who will bring on new adventures. They don't want to ask you, only to get the same response, "It's up to you" or "I am OK with whatever you decide". Throw something new out. If you are afraid of rejection for your idea, make another one. Eventually, you will all agree on something. But make a suggestion.

Did you know that being a *nice girl* could cause others to think this way about you? That you are weak, non-opinionated, dishonest, or untrustworthy? While you were out getting the job done and feeling valued, others gave you less value. You are trying to be nice and not hurt feelings, but you are coming across as a lying, insincere, spineless mess. Well, it's not all *that* bad, but you understand the point. You can try, but seldom will you ever please everyone.

Most people like someone they can count on, even if their feelings sometimes get hurt when someone is honest or says no. Many don't like people who are pushovers. They want people around them who have their own opinions and suggestions and will be straightforward when needed. This is not to say *nice girls* cannot be this way, but most need to work up to this. That is what you are going to be doing. You want to be nice but firm. You want to help but not be overworked. You want to be social but not used.

There is nothing wrong with being nice. You want to be nice in ways that benefit your health and well-being. To achieve this, you need to find the strength to make some changes. It won't be easy at first, but as you continue to work on these strategies, it will get easier and become a way of life.

The most important person should be *you*. You have given so much to everyone else. You have spent many hours giving your time and energy to your spouse, children, school, outside activities, employer, family, and friends. It is now time to start giving back to you. You deserve your time. You deserve your energy. This does not mean that you will not be giving to others. This does not mean that everything will come to a halt. But you will remove things from your life to make more room for yourself.

It also means prioritizing yourself when deciding to do things for others. This means considering whether what is being asked of you will also benefit you. It means you have the right to say no and not feel bad about doing so. It means you are ready for changes in your life, and now is the time to start.

It was discussed what kind of *nice girls* there are and where you might fit in. It was discussed how being a *nice girl* can have real health concerns. It was discussed how some *nice girls* are just trying to survive. It was also discussed how being a *nice girl* can have a negative impact on others. You know you need to change this. You cannot change who you are and your built-in characteristics, but you can change how you use your niceness.

So, let's get this mission started! Put your mind and heart into this so you can feel the progress you make as you go. With every change you put effort into, you will feel a sense of accomplishment that will keep you motivated to continue. When the times get tough, remember that you have a group of women in your shoes fighting the same battles. You may not see them or talk to them, but they are reading this book for the same reasons you are. You are not in this alone. You have the *nice girl* spirit flowing all around you, guiding you on this journey. Just be still and listen.

Alright, it's time to pull up those big girl pants, toughen up a bit, and power forward. Let's go!

Chapter Three

Find Your Courage

Taking a stand isn't a statement towards others but for yourself. ~TD

At this point, you have an idea that you are a *nice girl* and have decided to change. That you *need* to change. You don't want to change being a nice person, but you want to start living a life for yourself and not everyone else. That decision, alone, is courageous. This change in your life will be necessary and very powerful.

This will not be an easy task. Change can be challenging, even if it is for the good. Changing your actions and decisions will be not only for you but also for others around you. This may be difficult for others to adjust to, especially those who expect so much from you. Do not let this stop or detour you. Do not let it discourage you or set you back. Be willing to take on these challenges. Be encouraged to start a new life that allows your world to evolve around you instead of everyone else. Be empowered with every decision you make in your life.

Life should be exciting and fun. You want to be happy and make others happy. You do not want to sacrifice yourself to do this. You want to give freely and willingly. You do not want it to feel like a chore or an excruciating job. You do not want to hold resentment with anyone you help. You do not want to beat yourself up for not doing a good enough job. You do not want to push yourself to the point of sickness. What is the point of helping others if you aren't helping yourself?

Time to change! You can do this, and you will have support along the way. Others are going through this, too. Spiritually, there is much support and sisterhood. You have taken the first step and found the courage to change. This process may be difficult, but you are willing to push through. It is easy to give up and return to old ways and comfort zones. You do not want to do that, so you need to look deep inside yourself and know you are doing something that will benefit you in the long run. Wanting to change and taking action to do it are not the same. You must commit to this and know you are going in fully. So, let's feel that courage, take this stand, and begin!

This change will take place because you have hopes and dreams for yourself. You have goals in life that you want to accomplish for *you*. You can't take on everyone else's and keep putting yours on the side. It is time to take action in *your* life. You know this, you feel it, and you want it. But you are afraid. You are afraid to say no if asked for help. You are afraid you will be letting others down. You are afraid you will disappoint people. You are afraid of not being included. You are afraid of not being liked. You are afraid of being afraid. You can be afraid of everything, but the one thing you should be afraid of is not living for yourself. You should be afraid of not trying to fulfill your own dreams. You should be afraid of not living your own life to the fullest. You should be afraid of not changing. Feed your courage!

Use your courage to say no. Use your courage to stand up for your own life. Use your courage to have more time to spend with your family. Use your courage to be happy with your own goals. Use your courage to lose some people in your life (they were not real friends anyway if they don't support you on this journey). Use your courage to have time for vacations. Use your courage to do hobbies you want to start, continue, or complete. Use your courage to be strong. Use your courage to feel love for yourself instead of needing love from others. Use your courage to take the steps to live a life that is not overbearing. Use your courage to help others when you have time or want to, not because you feel you have to please them. Use your courage to stop pleasing others to fill unnecessary voids. You will be happier, fulfill your own life, and no longer have these voids.

This is your moment. This is your time to live for yourself. It is an excellent and liberating step to self-freedom. This does not make you selfish, greedy, a mean person, or even make you a bitch. It makes you a human being who has come to terms with the fact that you can only do so much for so many reasons before it is time to do something for the most important one… you!

If you find it hard to find your courage, re-read some of the reasons in this book on why you should. Use these words to encourage you to gain your courage and keep it. First, you must realize that it is okay to change. You need this change, and it is essential. You have the feeling that you cannot go on like this anymore. It is unhealthy for you physically and mentally. Realizing this is a considerable step towards reasons to change. Some people may never know they need to stop this behavior and will go until it takes them out dramatically. You may have come to this point, which is why you need to stop. Hopefully, you are changing before you get to that point. Either way, it is a great time to move in a different direction.

When you start to falter, look at what keeps you from finding your courage: fear. It would be expected to feel fear when changing your way of life. You will change as a person, allowing you to be there for yourself now. You will stand up for yourself and what you want. You don't know what the responses from others will be. You fear that you won't fit in, be needed, be available, be liked, and be included. These are all reasons we previously mentioned and are completely understandable fears. When you have had a particular way of life and have been a part of many groups, projects, or events, it will be a significant change to not have so much in your life anymore. When you start doing what is right for you and standing up for yourself, some won't like it. Some people will fade away. Some people may beg you to help, and the pressure might set you back. You may also find that you can be replaced, which will be painful. There are going to be challenges. That is all part of self-growth. But what you will lose will be replaced with so much more.

For the *nice girl* who isn't the kind that belongs to many organizations or events, but, instead, is the *nice girl* that is always there for someone who needs a shoulder, an ear, advice, a chauffeur, or a mom who has sacrificed herself for many years so others can have, these changes may be challenging. You are the ones who always have that smile for everyone, even when you might be hurt, too. You have selflessly given to others regularly and put yourself on the side. You have everyone's needs met while sacrificing your own. Mostly because others feed from your energy and never replenish you; they take, and you give. This could be family, friends, co-workers, and especially children.

You are going to find it hard to put yourself first. You will feel selfish and question whether this is what you should be doing. Yes! It is time for *you!* It is time that you take time for yourself. It is time you bought things that you want and need. It is time to spoil yourself with a manicure or pedicure. It is time for that new hairstyle. It is time to put a few new clothes in your closet. It is time to pull out that dusty exercise equipment and care for your body. It is time to plan that vacation, find a new job, or set new goals. It is time for you to start living life for yourself instead of others. There is nothing selfish about this. It is necessary for your body, mind, and spirit to keep you in fabulous condition.

You all have your own *nice girl* behaviors. Some may vary in ways from one another. The one sure thing you all need is change. You all need to start thinking of yourselves, and you all need to start taking steps to find the courage to change and follow through. You need to face your fear of change. You must face the fears you are building up and don't want to confront. Fear is a mental state. It means to be afraid or worried about something. Many times, our fear is false. The things we create in our minds often don't even happen. Fear is just a state that tries to hold you back. Don't let it. Don't give fear the satisfaction of controlling your life and stopping you from reaching your new life, goals, and dreams.

If some of your fears become reality, be brave enough to confront them. Handle the situations with dignity and courage. Instead of letting your fear hold you back, let it move you forward. Fear is an energizing source. Allow this energy to compel you into courageous action. It does not mean you are not afraid, but you are using the strength to move forward despite the fear. You know this is the right thing to do. Even if you are stepping into the unknown, you know these changes will make you a better person. When you feel nervous, it usually means you are on the path to better and bigger things. Taking your steps to move forward in fear is brave. When you know something is right, you move into it with nothing stopping you but you. Being afraid of change is expected. Pushing through is what makes you different.

When you question your ability to change your ways, remind yourself why you are doing this. Remind yourself of your dreams and goals in life. Remind yourself that you are worth your own time. Remind yourself that life is short, and you don't want to look back and wish you had done this but didn't. Remind yourself that you will have more time for other things you want to enjoy. Remind yourself that it is not worth keeping yourself in a life of stress and exhaustion. Remind yourself that you don't need to be used. Remind yourself that others can take care of themselves. Remind yourself that there is only one of you, and you need to be pampered, too. Remind yourself that you will always be a nice person, but you are just done being a *nice girl.*

Even if being the *nice girl* is wearing you down, and you find no comfort in it, it is still your comfort zone. You know what to expect and how things will happen for the most part. You know what you are in control of and what you aren't. You know how much time and effort are being taken from you, and you do not expect anything for yourself. Going outside of this comfort zone will be a new challenge. It will be hard for some to move outside of their set zone. Some of you are ready. Some of you have had more than enough and are moving on to bigger and better things. But some of you will hold on and make any change a battle that will be difficult to overcome.

Even when change is for the better, it can be challenging to push through. You don't like the unpredictable. You do not like having little to no control. To make this a better transition, find the courage to face this and move with the changes. Don't fight it. Don't keep looking back at what you had, but look forward to what you will gain. Keep your view ahead of what will be and not behind at what was. Focus on the direction you want to go.

When your courage to change your life starts to fade or becomes too difficult, focus on your dreams and desires. Your goals, wants, and needs are not just wishes and dreams; they are the essence of your life. Connect with what you truly want - go beyond just thinking about it and take action to achieve it. Connect these with your deepest values, bringing you a greater purpose to see you through these challenging times. Sometimes, you need to dig deep, but if you want it, you will find what you must do to get through.

Another way to maintain your courage for change is to view yourself in the future. Look five to twenty years ahead. Where do you want to be as a person and/or career? What do you want to accomplish? What sparks your passion for life? Are you working on these things? What do you need to do to get there?

Now, imagine you are that age in the future. Ask these questions: *Did you do everything you wanted? Did you see regrets for not taking a chance or taking a stance? Did you see yourself following what you want, or are you doing what others expect of you? Did you live your life for yourself or live it for everyone else? Did you fulfill your dreams, or did you continue to help others achieve theirs?* Now is the time to predict how you will answer these questions in the future.

You can still help others while fulfilling your dreams. You can be helpful and nice without letting yourself fall short. That is where you want to be and where you are going. You can work on that while transitioning in the direction of being nice without being the 'nice girl.' Being helpful and generous on your own terms is key. Finding the courage to say no, to achieve your own wants and needs, and to be empowered is essential. Getting there is the hard part, but once you are there, you will be so glad you did. Enjoy the journey along the way; this is where you grow.

Author's note: I have had to make many changes in my life. The big decisions have been scary, laborious, challenging, and uncertain. I always work on improving my life. Sometimes, deciding to change something is necessary to create better outcomes. Many of the hardest decisions have been the most positive, life-altering ones.

One that wasn't as difficult but required some soul searching was about a job. I had a great job that made me feel important. I worked for a city where I worked closely with the city council and elected officials, making important phone calls, gathering necessary information, and conducting important meetings that made me feel valued. I was a clerk at regular council meetings held every Tuesday night. I received calls after work hours to help councilmembers. I did a lot for the city, but it took me a couple of years to realize I wasn't there for my kids the way I wanted to be. Yes, I took them to practices, games, friends, and events. I was in the house with them, made them dinner, and did our daily routines, but I wasn't fully present. My mind was always somewhere else. Focusing on the next meeting, what work I had to get done, and how to fit everything in.

This is one of the problems with being a *nice girl*. They like pleasing everyone, and they enjoy feeling important. Important to people who they *think* appreciate it. But then I had to wonder, *who would really appreciate me more, the people who will pass through my life, or my children who will be a part of me forever?* It took me a while to realize that I was trying to be important to everyone at work, but I wasn't fully there for my kids, who are more important. Although I was always there for their needs, I lacked mental awareness, and that thought bothered me. And my kids could feel it, too. I had to change this. You may think I *am in the PTA for my kids and work in their classroom. I run the Cub Scouts and am the team parent for their sports, so I am very involved with my kids.* But how much time are you *really* spending with your kids and appreciating them when you are so busy with everything else? Are you giving to your kids or, instead, to those around them?

Don't take everything I say to heart. Not everything will apply to you. Some people can excel in multiple areas and have it all down pat. Most of us don't. Most of us try to push ourselves in so many directions that we can't focus on one—wasted energy with great intentions. Anyway, I felt I was being important to the wrong people in my life. I needed to work and be a good employee, but I also needed to be a mom. Sure enough, when I quit that job, I lost all association with the people I was so *important* to. That is how important I was to them. They filled the position with someone new; now, she is the important one. Being important is a feeling we perceive, but in many situations, it can be replaced.

When changing my situation to be there for my children, I didn't realize the adjustment would be so difficult. I had a hard time with the new transition. I got a new job with no evening hours. I was now working in a large county instead of a smaller city. I was in a public works department with almost a hundred other employees in the building. I went from being important in a small city to being just a number in a large county. I wasn't important here; I wasn't depended on. I was just an employee working eight hours a day and then going home. That's it. Nothing more. This was not good for me. Actually, it wasn't good for my ego.

I started to have thoughts that I wasn't important as a person. I wasn't worthy. I was just like everybody else. I was replaceable (which I understood from my last job). I wasn't special at all. Oh my gosh! I *am* unimportant! This is horrible. What have I done? I wanted to spend quality time with my kids, and all I was thinking about was what I had lost and how meaningless I felt. That was not what was supposed to happen. It was supposed to be freeing, beautiful, and fulfilling. Instead, it was quite the opposite. This was just a hot mess. One big hot mess!

I will admit that it took me about a year to appreciate just going to work and going home. I started to like not having calls at night. I liked just being an employee, and once work was over for the day, it was over. It was not a quick fix for me overnight. You would think it would have been easier for me since I made this change for a reason, but the feeling of self-value can be tremendous to some. It was more significant to me than I had realized. Kids don't come out and say how much they appreciate you. But then again, neither did my work. So, I had to get it together and realize what was important to me: my ego or my time with my children, being as important to them as I could be.

After a year or so of self-absorbed pity, I felt good. I loved not worrying about Tuesday night meetings or calls at home. This even allowed me to coach my daughter's softball team, which was an unexpected and welcome development. It had helped me overcome my slump of a failed marriage, feeling unimportant, and being a disappointment. This experience was so much more than just coaching a team. I didn't realize how much until one moment during our last game party. One of the parents came to me and told me that her daughter wanted to quit softball, but because of our team and me, she would continue to play. Because of me, she felt important when she didn't feel that on her previous teams. That is when it hit me: it wasn't about me being important;

it was about me making *others* feel important, including my children.

I thought I needed to be the important one. I thought I needed to be needed, which I do. We can all feel this way. We need to feel like we have value to others. However, I discovered during this process that it wasn't about being important at my job but being important enough to make those around me feel important because of the job I was doing for them. Not as a validation to fill some void, but because this is what makes me happy and feels good to me. This is who I am as a person. This makes me a better person for myself and those around me. Not a job to be important at, but human beings feeling good because of what I have to offer as a person myself. Had I not found the courage to change careers to a less important status, I would never have had time to coach, and I would never have discovered something amazing that I needed in my life.

Having the time to coach a softball team for one season gave me quality time with my children and an epiphany. What I was seeking was to make *others* feel important. By being the person I am, I can make my customers, co-workers, vendors, and department important. If I am good, then they are good. If I am good, then it reflects on me as a person. I am not my job or volunteer title, but rather how I am as a person in whatever I do, whether as a coach, volunteer, parent, partner, or anything else in life. Feeling good for myself while making others feel good is what makes me… me. This helps me feel fulfilled in my world, which also led me to my writing and helping others through my books. One change brought many changes for the better. One change brought on years of a ripple effect that was not the purpose of one change in life, but brought on many beautiful changes.

I know this sounds like I am trying to please others by being a *nice girl,* but that isn't the case. It isn't about pleasing others; it's about pleasing myself. Doing what was best for me led me to help others feel good about themselves, too. If I can help a little girl feel good about herself again, that is way more important than the many years I felt important for making a business call. Work will always be work, but people make up our lives. Feeding ourselves to others to get approval is not the same as finding real value in helping others. There is a *nice girl,* and then there is purpose. Plus, I got to spend more time with my children. My son helped out on the team, my daughter discovered she wanted to be a catcher (which she did amazingly for a few years after that), and I felt like a mom again.

I got somewhat deep with that. I wanted to share one of my experiences because you never know how finding the courage to change one thing in your life may bring more to the surface than you expect. It may seem easy to quit a few things, like the Cub mom or scorekeeper, but it can also be quite a change you may not be prepared for. If you need acceptance, prepare for an awakening that may take place. You may flow well and wonder why you waited so long, or you could struggle with the change and feel less of a person. This is with anything you change about yourself. Eliminating things from your life, saying no, focusing on your dreams, or anything out of your norm. If it gets too hard and you want to give up and give in to the comfort of your box, find your courage! Keep your courage! Don't lose your courage! It will be worth it. Remember, it took me a good year to adjust to some of those changes. Everything in life that is worth it to you is also worth the work to get there.

There can be many reasons why you are a *nice girl*. You may be seeking acceptance. You may be feeling the need to feel important. You may be afraid of rejection. You may be living in fear. There is one courage. One courage we must seek and hold on to during this process. Find it. Hang on to it. Do not let go! Keep going forward!

Chapter Four

When to Say Yes

When you say yes to others, make sure you are not saying no to yourself ~ Paulo Coelho

Do you have a difficult time saying *no? Nice girls* can barely say the word. It doesn't seem to fall into their vocabulary very well. Are you already getting anxious about the thought of saying no to some people? Why is *no* so difficult to say? Some feel that saying no is mean or selfish. How can you deny helping another person when asked? If you do not have any plans, it would be rude to say no. Sometimes, just the guilt of saying no is too much to bear. Some may not say no to avoid emotional stress. Some don't say no because they will be excluded. Maybe you don't say no because you won't be asked again if you do. Or you don't say no to keep peace and avoid an argument. It is just one tiny two-letter word that can cause *enormous* stress!

There are many reasons why *nice girls* do not say no. Only you know your true reason. Whatever it is, you know it is time to change this behavior. You are tired of being the *yes girl*. Putting the word, *no*, in your vocabulary doesn't make you weak, mean, or selfish. It makes you human. It makes you real. It makes you truly live. It makes you empowered. It gives you your life back. Saying no lets you show yourself how you want to live your life and what you want to do with it.

You are saying no so that you can better your life. You are saying no so you can have quality time with your family. You are saying no to make time to do other things you have been putting off. You are saying no so you can pursue your dreams. You are saying no so you can fulfill your goals. Do not let others make this about them. Do not let others make you feel guilty. Do not let others make you feel like you are letting them down. Do not let others try to persuade you. Be aware that some of this may happen. You need to stay strong and find the courage to keep going. You are changing for you, not them. They are not living your life. They may want input in your life, but they are not living it. You do what is best for you. You stay on the path you are heading on.

This book suggests that you say *no*. No, no, no! You know that is not going to be easy to do. The best way to start this process is by taking baby steps. You haven't been able to say no for many years, so you will not just start doing it tomorrow. Try to start saying no whenever something isn't good for you. Even the smallest no can help in this process. For instance, if you are on your way home to make dinner so you can head out to a school meeting, and your husband asks you to stop off at the dry cleaners, but you know it will make you late, say *no*. With your *no,* offer a small explanation that you do not have time, and he can do it today, or you can do it tomorrow. That is all you need to say. You do not need to feel guilty. You do not need to give five hundred reasons for feeling bad. You do not need to justify your reason for not doing it. This is what you do not do after saying no... *Oh, wow, now I feel bad. I should call him back and tell him I will. Why did I say no? Now I hurt his feelings. Now I feel bad for not doing it for him. If I am late, I must tell them something important came up. If I just told him yes, I wouldn't feel this way. But I don't want to be late for the meeting. That doesn't make me look good to the others. Ugh, I feel horrible. This is so much!* ... Stop! Just say *no!* It really can be simple if you let it be. It might take your husband back a little and put him in shock, but he will live. No one is dying because you said *no* to dry cleaning. (And if your partner or spouse is one of the reasons you are a *nice girl* out of fear and abuse, then please move out of that relationship and seek professional help!) But say no, you will get it tomorrow, and if he needs it now, he will need to go. That's it. Move on with life.

But if saying no is just too hard to do right now, then say *yes.* Start saying *yes* to the things that will benefit you. Some of us have it in our nature to say *yes* to others but not ourselves. Then you have people who say no to others but yes only to themselves. You may admire people who can say no and mean it. They say it, stick to it, and keep on moving. Since *nice girls* are not this way, the change may be easier if you stick to *yes.* This is a mixed message, but it will help with the change process. There are some essential things you need to say *yes* to.

Say yes to change. We cannot evolve if we continue to do the same things. We need to make some changes in our lives. This is about feeding our souls with new experiences. This is taking chances that will better your life and bring new adventures. This isn't about changing the sheets on the bed, but maybe you can start by changing your coffee order. Consider changing your hair or adjusting your daily routine by just one thing. Buy a different style of shirt. Small changes can lead to larger ones. Here's a thought: Maybe change your nice girl ways to simply being a nice *person.*

When you slowly start saying *yes* to new things in your life, it will be easier to start saying *no* to others. You are going to want to fill your life with good yeses. You will enjoy discovering parts of your life that you didn't know could exist. The *nice girl* has said *yes* to so many other people making their way, but now it is time to make your own way. Allow and make changes in your life that will open and expand your world. Change can be difficult and scary, but it can also be exhilarating. Flow through your changes instead of fighting them. Be open to them. Not everything will work for you, and that is OK. But you will not know if you don't try, so learn as you go. It doesn't have to be perfect; you need to keep going.

Change happens all the time, whether we realize it or not. But sometimes life can change dramatically in an instant. Nothing is wrong with you making changes to your life that will enhance your living. It's better to be the one making changes in your life than having others do it for you. So, be open to your change and flow with it!

Say yes to help. When you are tasked with many projects, and someone offers to help you, do you often say, "Thank you, but I got it," and later wish you had accepted it? Are you the *do-it-all* type of person? If the answer is yes, you need to change this. Start saying *yes* to help when it is being offered. There is no weakness or shame in allowing others to help you. It is doing them justice by assisting you. You are allowing them the joy of being helpful. You are giving them the gratification of being a part of something, just like how you like being a part of something. It is not about you being Wonder Woman; it is about letting others be allowed to participate and you not hogging it all. Share the work and let others get satisfaction from feeling valuable, too.

When other people offer to help you, whether they are sincere or not, let them. Say *yes,* even if it is something simple that you could do yourself. Every little bit you give to someone else frees up more time for you. This is your goal. You want to have more quality time for your family, friends, and especially yourself.

You know that feeling of accomplishment, praise, appreciation, and importance you get from doing so much for others? Of course you do. You are a *nice girl.* It makes you feel good. By allowing someone else to help you, you pass that feeling onto them. Why be selfish with this? If you are supposed to be nice, then you need to be nice and share. You should allow others to feel these emotions, too. Do not think you are setting them up to fail. Many people are not *nice girls.* They only want to help with a portion of something and be done with it. They won't continue to carry a *nice girl* torch, so give them something to help with. Let them feel good for that moment while freeing yourself to move on to other things. Unless you absolutely are the only one who can do the work, say *yes* to help.

Say yes to time with family and friends. You might feel that you have been spending quite a bit of time with them already. You have been spending time with your kids at their school functions. You are spending time with them at sports activities. You see your friends at these events and hang around and chat, or you see friends every day at work. Maybe you text friends and family daily, so you communicate regularly. That's great! But where is your quality time?

Getting significant quality time with those you care about is very important. This is a time when you are not at events. This is a time when you are not in a hurry to get on to something else. This is a time when you are relaxed, having fun, and simply enjoying each other's company. Quality time is giving one's undivided attention to strengthen a relationship. That relationship can be lovers, friends, or family. Even a stranger. It is undivided attention.

Do you have family game nights? Just sitting around a table having fun with no technology, but music playing in the background. Game nights are not for everyone. Many can't seem to fit that length of time in, but if you are willing to, it can be a great time spent together. You can have a movie night if you are not into games, but it is preferred that you do something where you speak to each other and communicate.

You could go on a family hike, picnic, outdoor adventure, or spend a night in the backyard in a tent. If you are not the outdoor type, you can have a house project day, bowling, indoor golf, or a nice family dinner out. If everyone is a little older and doing their thing, one night a week, have a sit-down dinner together. Just remember to turn off your technical devices during this time. Connect with humans and not with phones or other devices. Fill each other in on what is going on in your lives. We all want our privacy, but we also need to share with our families what our world is like around us.

When was the last time you visited family and enjoyed it? Parents, siblings, children, aunts, uncles, and cousins. Life gets busy, and we often put off family gatherings until months pass, or sometimes even years. If you're not the type of family who gets together frequently, you should add family time to your 'yes' list. We tend to think we have all the time in the world to put them off and see them later, but we shouldn't do this. Find the time to reconnect and feel that bond of family ties with you.

Plan a day to drive and spend quality time with family members. Take the opportunity to talk, laugh, eat, drink, and enjoy each other's company. While you can still communicate through phone calls, video chats, texts, and regular conversations, nothing beats face-to-face time, ending with a good hug. Make this a priority on your schedule and alternate your time with each family member to see them all. You don't want time to slip away.

Spending time with friends is essential. You may spend time with many people you know, but is it quality time? Don't use this time to be busy; use this time to talk. Use this time to engage in real conversation. Use this time to have friend time, have fun, and enjoy each other's company. Even if you have a couple of friends over for dinner or a night out, use it as a fun time. Of course, you will probably talk about the kids and things coming up, maybe work if you are co-workers, but don't focus on that. Focus on what you are doing and be in the moment, experiencing human bonding. Meet for lunch, shopping day, or just a coffee. Maybe an adventurous outing is in order. Do something fun that doesn't include other events, such as kids' activities or work. There is something about spending time with people, being with them, and not having any other agenda.

Say yes to new experiences and adventures. New adventures are fun and bring out inner goodness in your soul. They make you feel more alive. What some would call adventures, others wouldn't. This isn't about a major mountain climbing event, although that could be extraordinary, but rather simple adventures considered unknown territory, and getting out of your box. These adventures have nothing to do with helping others or joining a new group function event. They are experiences and actions that are all about doing something for you. It can be taking a spa day, a friend shopping day, a coastal drive, skydiving, or a seven-day cruise. Whatever would be considered an *adventure* to you, do it. Connect yourself to other activities that don't involve planning, scorekeeping, or doing for others. Do activities that expand yourself and push you outside of your comfort zone.

Author's note: Being a single, busy mom of three, I was going in many directions. I was working to live, but living for my kids. Everything revolved around their events and schedules. As they got older, I knew I needed to do some things for myself. I fear heights, but decided to go to an adventure park with my oldest daughter. This place had high ropes and a wire to walk on with a small zipline. To some, that may seem like child's play with no adventure at all. To me, it was like I had conquered Mount Everest. This experience was the opening to many more things to come. I love trying new things now and doing things for myself. I love expanding and pushing the limits I have set for myself. I even went with my daughters on a parasailing adventure. I can't say I would do it again, but I did it, and it opened my soul to conquer so much more because of the courage I found to do it. Find out what adventure is to you and do it. And then do another! —*end of author's note.*

Getting out of your comfort zone builds your inner strength. Gather the courage to do something in the unknown, knowing it will pay off in the long run. Taking that risk to break your barrier can lead you in new directions and open your soul to freedom and independence. You just have to do it.

Say yes to goals. When was the last time you set goals for yourself? A goal that you want to achieve but have been putting off or given up on. A new goal that you didn't know until this moment that you wanted to achieve. A goal that will get your fire burning for *you.* Goals can be amazing life changers. They may not change the outside world, but to your inner self, they can change everything.

Author's note: One of my biggest goals was to write a book. I had the thought since the sixth grade, but I put it off for many years. Finally, at forty, I was ready to act on this goal. And I did! It did not just happen overnight. It wasn't something that just came to me, and it wasn't always easy. It took me five years to write. I was a single mom of three children, and life had to take precedence. I would write and take a few months off. I would write and take another few months off. But I didn't give up. It just took longer than I wanted. Then, it took a couple more years to publish my book because it took a while to go through the editing process. I honestly could not believe I accomplished that goal when it was for sale online. It was surreal for a while. Even now, I am still amazed, but it has set a course for me because here I am writing this book, too!

I have many goals, but one significant one I want to accomplish is to publish the first book I started writing. That's right. I didn't complete the very first book I started writing. My first book was fictional, and it's still not complete; I am still working on the first chapter. During the writing process, something turned my course into motivational, self-improvement writing. I completed my goal of writing a book. I am a published author; it just wasn't where I started. The goal I accomplished did not change the world, but it has changed me. I will finish the very first fiction book because, even though I had a detour, I won't quit! – *end of author's note.*

Doing something that has such meaning to you opens you up and gives you wings. The journey towards reaching a goal is a learning experience. It also provides strength and freedom to your soul. It builds character and helps you evolve. When you accomplish your goal, it is a celebration that involves many emotions. It is something you do for you. You deserve this for all your hard work. You spend so much time helping others achieve their goals that it is time for you to achieve goals for yourself. Write down what you want to achieve and take steps to make that happen. Every day, do a little something to help reach that goal.

Say yes to hobbies. People underestimate hobbies. Many people don't have the time for hobbies. Since you will be releasing projects to others or eliminating them and getting help from others, you should have more time to devote to this. If you have been wanting to do this or putting it off, now is the time. Not everyone will be able to or should fill their time with hobbies.

You should say *yes* to hobbies if you are having difficulty with extra time on your hands, and you have been wanting to do them. If you feel the urge to jump back into your *nice girl* mode because you feel like you are wasting time not being fully busy, you are not feeling valued doing less, or if you need something to occupy your mind and hands, try a hobby. Additionally, some hobbies can be social and allow you to be part of something without the demands that often accompany them. Hobbies may not seem like a big deal compared to people pleasing, but when you start doing things for yourself, no matter how small, they build up.

Take some time to read for thirty minutes a day. Make items you could sell or give as gifts for family and friends. It could be anything—painting, sculptures, models, cooking, baking, or gardening. Maybe practice for a timed run. Let it be yours. Your time, your activity, your thing! Once you start taking time to do hobbies, you will realize how much doing things for yourself holds as much value, if not more, than doing things for others. It is nice to please your own heart, too.

You may not expect much from a hobby, but that is okay. Just doing something that you enjoy is all you need. Other ideas could be photography, making wood signs, or painting rocks. Maybe you would like to hike or kayak. You can bake something new each week, refurnish furniture, or do crossword puzzles. It doesn't matter what your hobby is, but it must fulfill your soul and well-being. It doesn't need to lead to future endeavors, but if it does, go with it. Enjoy it! But ensure it does not get overwhelming and remains a hobby benefiting you, not depleting you. The idea is for fun and fulfillment.

Say yes to yourself. This is the biggest *'yes'* you will ever do. *It's* the most important one. Whatever comes your way that will benefit you and your life, say *yes*. You may think being the new classroom mom president will benefit you, but will it? Will it take time away from the things you want? Is it to help your ego? We all want our egos to be rubbed nicely now and then, but we need to know when to say *yes* to our well-being and not a boost of approval.

You want to say *yes* to things that benefit you, not those around you. You have been saying *yes* to others rather than yourself for years. Now, it is time to say *yes* to you. Now is the time to start doing things that are about you. Now is the time to make changes for you. You are living your life. You need to say *yes* to things that will help you grow. You need to say *yes* to things that will keep you from toxic people and situations. You need to say *yes* to things that fill you up with goodness. You need to say *yes* to things that you have been wanting to do but have been putting off because you have been too busy helping everyone but yourself. Now is the time to say *yes* to you!

This can also be a time of saying *no*. Saying *yes* to yourself can be saying *no* to others. If you are saying *yes* to yourself about that one hour of quiet time you desperately need, you might be saying *no* to running errands or working extra hours on projects. If you are saying *yes* to that lunch date with a friend you have been putting off for months, you might be saying *no* to a PTA function. If you are saying *yes* to a new job opportunity you have been wanting, you might be saying *no* to current co-workers you will not be associating with anymore. If you say yes to spending more time with your family, you might say *no* to your phone. Your yeses will outweigh what is being said no to in your life. It may be difficult sometimes, but know that you will be better as time goes on. And real friends will understand and not abandon you.

These yeses will be your hardest yeses to say, but your most important. When you say *yes* to things that benefit your life, it can lead to even bigger decisions of yes in the future. You will be benefiting your well-being. For example, if you are in a toxic relationship, this can be the time to say *yes* to yourself and leave. If your job has been emotionally and physically draining, this is when you say *yes* to a new job or opportunity. If you want to move but feel that the change is too scary, this is when you say *yes* to a new living place. If you have been hiding behind closed doors but want to get into the world, this can be the time you say yes to yourself and find some newfound freedom.

All of the yeses are important for you and your life. It is important to care for others. It is important to help others. It is important, at times, to put others in front of you. It is also essential to say *yes* to you. It is not selfish. It is not bad. It is not terrible. It is a necessity.

If you have a hard time with these, start small. Just focus on one thing at a time. You can start by saying *yes* to family and friends for a month. Plan out time to be with them or give them your undivided attention when in their presence. The following month, start doing something new. You can try a new haircut or join a yoga class. Then, in the next month or two, you can add a goal you want to focus on. Write down your goal and ten things you can do to achieve it. Set out time daily to focus and work on that goal. If you still have open time or busy hands, the following month, add a hobby. This one is not a must, but it can open a different side of you that is fun and stress-relieving. Hobbies can be very therapeutic. Finally, say *yes* to everything that benefits you; do it!

This will be a process. It will not happen in a day. It may not occur in a few months. You might have to wait until new people take new positions. For example, if you are on the PTA Board and no longer want to be on it, you may need to wait until the next election to be removed. If you are a scorekeeper for your child's team, you may need to wait until the season ends. You don't want to quit everything and leave others high and dry. You are classy, and you walk away with dignity. However, if you are in a position where you need to let go of things now, find a replacement and let someone else take it over. If there is someone else who is willing to do the job for you, let them. Again, you are sharing and letting them feel important, too. You are nice enough to do that. If you need to wait to let go of something, work on other areas during this time.

Just a reminder, this is not about letting go of *everything* in your life. If you want to be the room mom, be the room mom. If you want to work on the fundraisers, work on them. If you want to take on extra projects at work, do it. You are eliminating extra things that are not benefiting you.

You are removing things that are becoming burdensome. You are getting rid of things that are not good for your well-being. You are eliminating things that no longer suit you. You can still be a part of things, but minimize it. Don't be Super Mom or Wonder Woman. Don't be the *go-to girl*. Don't be used and tossed around. However, if something still works for you, stick with it. Just make sure you are doing it for you. And remove yourself from the ten other things that don't make you as happy.

Don't force too many yeses on yourself as you make these changes. You need to start your *yes* process slowly, avoiding overexertion that can become overwhelming. We are trying to fix a problem, not create a new one. Just remember to ask yourself, is this a benefit or a burden? If it benefits you, then it is a *yes*. If it is a burden or stresses you, say *no*. Even if it may benefit you, it can become a burden if you have too much going on, defeating the purpose of what you're trying to accomplish. Think carefully before making decisions and ensure they will work in your favor. If it doesn't work for you, pass! If it will enhance, lift, benefit, or make you happy, say *YES!*

Simply put, a woman in her thirties said she used to say yes all the time. It bothered her, and one day, it hit her, making her realize that she needed to stop. She now sees it as a sign that if any situation bothers her in any way, and if she is only saying yes to benefit the person asking, then that is when she needs to say no.

You may feel guilty, stressed, and/or anxious about saying no, but look at it this way: you are saying the word no to them, but you are saying yes to you. In time, it will become easier. The stress of saying yes to yourself will outweigh the stress of trying to do everything for everyone else, and some things that you don't want to do anyway. If you want to do it, do it. If you aren't doing it with peace in your heart, then don't! Make it that simple.

Chapter Five

Work That Schedule

The key is not to prioritize what's on your schedule, but to schedule your priorities. ~Stephen Covey

For many years, you have scheduled your life around others. For many years, you have tried to live at a pace that was just reachable, but it has pushed you to your limits. Those limits are either now met, or you are getting close. You know you need to change this pattern. The *nice girl* has had her adventure. You have participated in different activities, met various people, and had many experiences. The *nice girl* is also worn out emotionally and physically. You have played into others' lives while neglecting yours. You have filled your days accommodating others while putting yourself on the side. Now, the *nice girl* needs to be set aside so you can redirect yourself and focus on how you spend *your* time.

This change in your lifestyle will open up your calendar, giving you freedom in areas you have not had for a long time or never before. This may be scary. What do you do with your time? What will keep you occupied? What will help you feel important? At this time, you may consider returning to your old ways, as the comfort zone sounds more appealing than the unknown. But don't! Everything takes time. Just breathe and have some patience while you are redirecting your path. You will still be busy, but in a different way. Your time will still be valued, but now it will be for you.

If you had a job taking up too much of your time and took a new job that freed up some time, make your extra time about you. If you ended a relationship with a lover, family member, or friend who was taking up so much of your time, this time is now about you. It isn't just about being busy with kids, events, or activities. Many things can pull you away from yourself and suck the time right out of you. You can also make yourself busy for no real reason other than the need to feel busy and wanted. You can be wasting your own time. You can be busy doing nothing. So, stop that, too! Don't be 'scattered busy', not accomplishing anything but filling time; focus on getting things done and eliminating what is not valuable for you. Now that you are getting some time back, make it count. Make it meaningful.

Many of us live with schedules. If you have children, you might have a calendar with so many marks that you can barely tell what day it is. If you work in business, your schedule can be filled with meetings. Some people have so many things going on that they write on Post-its and stick them on everything to avoid forgetting essential must-dos.

Schedules are important to keep your life in order and under control. The only concern with your schedule is what you are scheduling.

You schedule many things, and you work hard to get your list checked off. You schedule appointments. You schedule events that you should attend. You schedule return calls or follow-ups. You schedule when to place orders or when packages should be received. You schedule a variety of stuff to keep your life in check. With all of this scheduling, are you scheduling for your well-being? Are you scheduling time for yourself? Are you scheduling time that will benefit your life and feed goodness to your soul? This should be your priority.

When scheduling your life events, make sure to schedule time for you. If you need help in this area, here are some suggestions to focus on:

Schedule time to be alone. Many people do not like to be alone. Being alone can be scary. The quiet can be too loud. Many *nice girls* do not like being alone, so they are so busy being involved with everything. On the other hand, some *nice girls* may prefer to be alone because it gives them a break from having or wanting to be nice or busy. Some people want to escape from everything and avoid what is happening in the outside world. Then others are alone so much that they do not need any more alone time. They want to spend time with people. We are not all the same, and being alone can be a blessing or a burden. Use this alone time in ways that will benefit you.

Being alone can be a very calming and healing time. Don't take time alone to isolate yourself and run away from life. Take time alone to relax, replenish, and heal yourself.

This is not to say you are injured or sick. Healing can be anything from clearing the mind and resting your brain from outside sources to taking a nap to heal your tiredness. Being alone is a time when you can reflect and replenish your inner soul. You can slow down the outside noise and listen to the inner self. Some people want to avoid this. They like outside distractions. Some people don't want to hear what the inner self says. It doesn't want the truth. Listening to the inner self is a good thing to do. It is good to learn to hear what it has to say. Use this voice to help you say yes to things that benefit you. When you hear your inner voice, instead of all the outside sources, you are reminded of who you are and what *you* want.

Being alone also allows you to be more productive. By resting, listening, and slowing down, you gain insight, which can enable you to problem-solve, become more creative, and enhance your thinking abilities. Many authors and artists are known to retreat into seclusion to gather their thoughts and work productively on their projects. The lack of outside distractions pulls you closer to your full potential and abilities. Use alone time to benefit you and your life.

Being alone can also improve your relationships with others. When you are constantly around others, you can be influenced by their thinking. Spending time alone allows you to bond with yourself and discover what you truly want. By doing this, you become and remain your own person. Being yourself when around others is a bright light in the relationship. These relationships can be with family, friends, or partners. When you are true to yourself, you enhance what you bring to that relationship. Find time to connect with your inner self, behaviors, and wants out of other relationships.

Even in the strongest family and loving relationships, we must find our own space and outlets. There is nothing wrong with this. Finding alone time to bring yourself back to your own being is healthy and natural. Enjoy it.

During your alone time, you will find what you want in your life. During this time, you will hold yourself to your commitment to change. During this time, you will hear what is most important to you. During this time, you will find peace. During this time, you will find enlightenment. During this time, you will discover hidden parts of you that you want to bring out. Enjoy it all. Embrace being alone. You can take fifteen minutes, an hour, an entire day, a week, or when needed. However it works for you, do it. Every bit of this time is special and matters. Use your alone time to rediscover who you are and what you want in your life.

Schedule time to spend with family and friends. This has been discussed previously, so it will not be covered in detail here. This reminder encourages you to give undivided attention to your family and friends. Do you find it rude when you are talking to family and they are staring at their phone? People often say they are listening but are focused on their devices. Avoid this behavior. Give your full attention to others. It's not just about devices, but also about the surroundings. Don't be looking at other people or things, letting your mind wander, or thinking about what must be done later that day or tomorrow. Just focus on the current situation and the person or people you are with.

It is good for others to know you are paying attention to them. Just because you are making changes in your life for yourself doesn't mean you can't make others feel special while doing this. Let them feel important in your presence.

Even if you think you are not getting the same attention, give them yours. Spend time with family and friends to gain support for the changes you want to make. Your faithful supporters will come out during this time. These are the people you will want to focus on and keep in your future schedules. Also, if someone is not giving you their full attention, it is OK to let them know and ask them to pay attention to you.

Schedule time for activities. You made a decision to change. You are going to be doing more activities for yourself. The previous chapter discussed saying yes to activities. Now is the time to schedule some new things in your life. Now, the real fun begins. And it should be fun! No work activities. No activities for functions, organizations, or businesses. This time is set out for just plain fun. You can schedule things you have been putting off, such as movies, theatre, or musicals. It can be hiking, biking, or kayaking. It can be a camping trip, beach vacation, or cruise. Anything that will take you away from work and other duties so you can relax and enjoy. And maybe get that adrenaline going!

This activity time is meant to be for you. You can do your activities alone, with friends, family, or whoever you choose. You can schedule the same activities regularly or pick new ones each time. This is a fun time. Enjoy your *life* time. Your *be adventurous* time. This is where you bring excitement back into your life. This is where you can let loose and be free. This is where you bring back bits of yourself that you have been leaving behind. This is where your explorer side gets filled. Whatever you use to fill this time, really enjoy it. You might try something and find that it isn't for you. That is OK. It wasn't a waste of time. If you had not tried it, you wouldn't know you didn't care for it. If you find something you like, do it again. You want to keep it fresh, but doing something you enjoy is the plan. If you like kayaking, that will be a repeated activity. You can try new places or maybe join a group. Just play with it and have fun.

You don't need to be a *really* adventurous person. Maybe you can go for a walk on a new trail. Many cities are getting paved walking trails in their areas. Take a walk in nature, out in the woods, or by water. Or take a bike ride. If movement is not your style, you can visit a new restaurant, a wine tasting, or a movie theater. The idea is to get out and do something fun that you can enjoy. Everybody needs to have some activity to do. It doesn't have to be all the time or incredibly drastic, but it does need to be something. Expand your horizons and feed your soul with fun goodness. You won't grow and will start to wither if you don't bring excitement and adventure into your life. Get out there and have some fun! Live life fully!

Schedule time to exercise. There are already some moans and some applause. This is one of the better activities to do for yourself. This should be at the top of your list of things to do. But…here comes the excuses. *I don't have time. I am too tired. I don't have money for a gym. I don't have exercise equipment at home. Blah, blah, blah.* It is just excuses. Why is exercise one of the more challenging things to do for yourself when it is one of the best things you can do? Chapter 6 will get into this more, but get up, put on those workout shoes, and do something for now. Give yourself at least fifteen to thirty minutes of exercise daily or at least a few days a week. This is your time for yourself. Don't take this for granted. Focus on taking care of yourself— you have one body for this one life. Take care of it.

Schedule time to accomplish goals. Goals are essential to have in your life. Everyone should be reaching some goal. Some people don't make goals because goals take work. They don't want to put that much effort into something. Some people do not want to set goals due to the fear of failure. They don't want to waste their time on it if it doesn't happen. They do not want to be let down. Answer this: *how do you know if you do not try?* If one goal is not reached, it may lead you on a different and better path. So, do not give up.

There is persistence and accountability if you make goals. Goals can range from easy to complex. It can take a few minutes if your goal is to get the house clean before leaving for work, or it can be years if you are trying to start your own business. Either way, it is something to strive for. It is something to accomplish and feel good about all of your progress.

Schedule time each day to work on your goals. If it is important to you to eat healthier, use time to plan and prepare your healthy meals. If a goal is to write a book, schedule thirty minutes to an hour a day of writing. If you want to invent a product, work on research and take steps to get it on the market. If you want to take a family trip to Disneyland, focus on your budget and save a portion of each paycheck.

You may not *work* on your goal every day, but rather work towards it. Some goals will require daily action, while others will require weekly work, or less. Just take the time to work on them and not put them off because something else came up. Goals can easily get sidelined while we live our lives, which is why many never get accomplished or reached. Make this one of your highest priorities. When you accomplish it, the time and effort will be worth it.

Schedule non-tech time. Technology has advanced significantly, and it's incredible how much things have evolved in recent years. Cell phones, the internet, apps, flat screens, and substantial social media have developed rapidly in recent years. With so much available, there is little effort to disconnect from the physical world. At the click of a button, there is so much information that you can find in seconds. The world keeps evolving. Many changes happen regularly. New ideas become reality and bring more technology for us to use. Sometimes, it can be overwhelming. Sometimes, it can be consuming. Sometimes, we must turn it all off and return to basics.

There is nothing wrong with going basic in the world of technology. Taking a break and returning to nature, manual work, or seeing someone in person instead of talking to them on a device is perfectly fine. Bringing yourself back to human awareness, rather than relying on a screen, is a beneficial practice. You would be doing yourself a favor by centering yourself on being human, which would also help your health and senses. It is good to drop technology for a bit and just be with *you!*

It can be challenging to let go of technology, as it is a massive part of our daily lives. You can do spurts of time-outs or a more extended absence. For instance, you can schedule thirty minutes a day without technology. You can walk and listen to what is happening around you instead of listening to your playlist. You can read an actual paper book, not an iPad. You can shop in the local markets instead of online. You can meditate in silence and listen to your inner self. This is not the same as giving them your undivided attention when you're with family and friends. This is a purposeful break from technology to work on yourself. Focus on you. Technology can hinder these changes because you may swap things for others. Give yourself real time.

Life revolves around technology, but studies have shown that breaking away from it is necessary to help you as a human being. These breaks will assist you in gaining focus in real-time, brain clarity, and human connection. They also help with sleep and productivity. You are scheduling quality into your life, so focus on activities requiring little technology. Although it may not be easy to live without it permanently in today's society, taking breaks is beneficial. It will help you gain more time to focus on your surroundings.

Schedule productive time. Planning time to be productive is an energy booster. Being productive rids you of the excess weight of burdens you can carry around on your shoulders. Do you feel good when you complete tasks? It could be cleaning a room, redecorating a kitchen, refurbishing a dresser, organizing a closet, or whatever you choose. Keep up with your environment so you won't be overwhelmed by your surroundings. Keep items organized and easily accessible. This will allow you to be more productive in other areas of your life and give you more time where you're needed or wanted. Being productive is not just busy work. In this process, being productive is making progress or finishing something you want accomplished. For example, you may have a room you want to remodel.

Complete this by scheduling time to look for and purchase paint. Schedule time to shop for new decorations. Schedule time each day to work on the space. Enjoy your accomplishments. Be proud of yourself and what you do. There is time in the production process, but what you get after the completion is well worth it.

You can always start a hobby if you don't have any projects to do. Let your productive time be rewarding but not overbearing. It's your time, and it should not be a source of grief but rather a productive fulfillment. You can engage in home crafts or take classes. You can blog, create or listen to a podcast, or dedicate one room a month to organization. Just do something that will give you satisfaction. It can be something small that no one will notice, but it can also be something you receive significant recognition for. Whether it is a hobby, specific chores, or personal time for yourself, feel satisfied and enjoy it.

Author's note: I enjoy making quilts and taking photographs. The quilts I make are primarily for family. They are not professionally made with a fancy machine; instead, they are made out of love, as it's my special time to be productive. I do it for fun, relaxation, stress relief, and alone time. I go into my room, turn up the music, and get started. I enjoy this time and love that I am making something and not wasting time. I enjoy seeing my family like and using them. Seeing the finished result always makes me feel good, even if it isn't perfect – *end of author's note*.

These suggestions, listed above and throughout the book, are just that: suggestions. Do what you want and what feels right for you, so that you can prosper in your life during these changing times. Remove or add anything that you think will improve your life, or focus on what you want to prioritize.

To meet some of these schedules, you may need to adjust some of what you have or change some of your daily routines to accommodate them. If you want to exercise, you may need to get up thirty minutes earlier. If you keep the same amount of sleep, you must change your schedule to go to bed thirty minutes earlier each night. Scheduling certain things may require some shuffling around. You should be used to this since you have been shuffling around to help others for many years. Now, you will be shuffling to meet *your* needs.

These items listed above are just examples. You can add or delete what will serve you better. You can focus on friends if you don't have family nearby. You can also schedule a call with far-away family members and connect via voice instead of typed words in a text. Arrange your schedule so that it works for you. It is important to schedule things in your life that will better yourself. Changing your routine may be difficult at first, but keep it going. Don't let a little frustration steer you off course. Usually, when things are uncomfortable or difficult, it is worth it.

Chapter Six

Clean Your Soul

As I unclutter my life, I free myself to answer the callings of my soul.

~Dr. Wayne Dyer

There is something about *spring cleaning* that inspires many people to purge. Spring is a time of renewal and awakening. It is a time to clean, renew, and refresh our surroundings. Although it is *spring cleaning*, it can be done any time of the year to help you gain control of your surroundings. It feels good to lessen the loads you carry. Many people on social media post pictures of their before-and-after experiences of cleaning and organizing. The change feels freeing and uplifting. It can, however, be messy and time-consuming during the process. It takes patience and some physical labor. But it is rewarding when completed and worth every ounce of hard work.

If you have clutter, schedule time to clean this up. Cluttered surroundings can bring on extra personal stress and anxiety. Studies have found that when people remove clutter from their lives, they have more energy, creativity, and calmness. Keep your life organized with files, storage bins, and labels. Get rid of extra items that you don't use or need. Donate them to charity or a family in need. Any extra clutter takes away from your energy space and can limit you emotionally. Open your space and gain energy by releasing that stress.

You are in a transitional phase. It will not be overnight that you stop helping everyone and sit down without a care in the world except what flavor of ice cream to eat. It seems like too much work to focus on yourself. Don't let it feel so tiresome. It can be pretty straightforward. Once things fall into place, it will just flow. Just focus on each day as it comes. You are changing to better yourself and your surroundings, and find freedom. You don't want to be a prisoner of your own space when you finally free yourself from others. We are not talking hoarders here, but maybe just clothes you don't wear, items you do not use, things thrown in a corner chair or the closet, or spare rooms that turned into storage. The little things can feel like big things when they tie you down.

You do not need to tackle your entire house at once. You can tackle a room a week or even a section a month. Little changes make a big difference, like cleaning out your junk drawer or installing organizing trays to make finding specific items easier.

You are already making many changes to your life that will benefit you. These changes may be challenging to implement. However, you may not always see the physical or emotional results that have occurred, making it difficult to gauge your progress on this journey. When you make changes, you will get a boost from your accomplishments, encouraging you to keep going. You will feel closer to the benefits of these changes taking place.

Start with something easy, go through your dresser and closet. Donate clothes to a local charity such as a domestic violence or homeless shelter. Declutter your bathroom and clean the counters, drawers, and cupboards. Get rid of unused lotions and perfumes you keep lying around. Throw away old make-up or ones you don't use. Fit everything under the counter or in drawers, leaving your countertops clean and open. Straighten up that plasticware cupboard in your kitchen and sort the bowls with the lids. Give your donation store all those coffee cups that are just taking up space. Put your craft and holiday items in labeled bins and stack them nicely in a designated area. File the papers lying around on your desk or kitchen counters. Also, keep your file system well organized. Don't just throw it all together into a mess.

If you want to do more, do some deep cleaning. Get behind the toilet and in the wall corners. Sweep out the closets and vacuum under the cushions. Clean out the car and put in an air freshener. Keeping your space clean keeps your mind free with less anxiety and stress. Of course, life happens, and we get stressed. However, any reduction in stress goes a long way. Decluttering your space is a benefit that people do not think much of. People get used to the way things are, just like in our daily lives. Let's go for the gusto when making changes to better your lives. Clean up your space! Continue to do this until you feel your space is open, free, and satisfying.

This *spring cleaning (or fall, winter, or any other time of year)* isn't just about cleaning up your surroundings. It is also about cleaning up your physical and emotional self. Maintaining good working order is essential, which includes avoiding drama, extra anxieties, and stress. You need a positive flow in your life, which means detoxing from negative influences. This can be a more complicated process. Physical strength isn't required to clean this area; inner strength is. This can be more draining, confusing, and exhausting. Ultimately, you will feel more accomplished and fulfilled than you have in a long time, so don't give up!

This is your chance to eliminate anything that does not feed positive energy into your life. If you have people or activities draining you, or you are draining yourself through self-neglect, this is the time to make a change. You are doing so well with your changes, so let's keep going.

De-clutter your friend list. This list would include friends *and* family. This is where it gets very challenging. You don't want to hurt anyone's feelings or have anyone upset with you. You will watch negative posts fly around on your social media pages and bring down your positive vibes, so that you won't hurt *their* feelings. Why? What makes their feelings or emotional status more important than yours? Do you see these people in person or just online? Would they be there in the middle of the night if you called them for help? Think about that. Many find their self-worth nowadays based on the number of *likes* or followers they have on social media. This is not who you are.

If you cannot delete negative and toxic people right now, then at least consider snoozing, unfollowing, or hiding them. If you didn't miss them or you feel better after not seeing them for a month, it's time to delete them. It may hurt for a bit, but you will recover. Feeling better about your connections, having positive conversations, and better well-being are more important now.

These relationships are not just the online unfollow and unfriend people in your life. They are also the in-person relationships you have that are pulling you down, feeding negatively into your soul, and draining you of energy. Limit contact with these people in your life if you are unwilling or unable to remove them permanently. But removal would be the best choice to make.

Detox your technology. Yes, even the technology you rely on can be draining you. Are you receiving many emails from the same sender that you delete and never open? Unsubscribe. Do you have a trillion apps on your phone that you never use? Delete them. Do you have numerous contacts you have never contacted? Remove them. When unused or unneeded items clutter your surroundings, it can feel like a thousand things weighing you down when it is only a handful. Remove or delete what you do not use, need, or want in your life instead of letting it linger around, taking up space.

If you need to unplug from social media for a little while to focus on some of the changes you're working on, do it! It is hard not to be connected, but sometimes you may need that break to focus on yourself, your life, and your inner peace. This is not a permanent solution; a week to refocus and get more time for yourself is a great idea. This is mentioned a few times because technology can hinder many lives and take up much of your time. Take breaks!

When you clean up your house and surroundings, you will also want your body and emotions clean. The body is your shell – your soul's house, so take care of it. It is your *place*. Just like your house, you need your body space to be clean.

Here are a few great ways to clean your body:

Drink water. You probably get tired of hearing this, and water is so dull, but it is necessary. Many people do not drink the daily recommended amount. If plain water is hard for you to drink, add lemon, cucumber, or raw fruits. Many different flavors can be added. While plain water is best, it's crucial to drink it. Your body relies on water to stay healthy and clean. And no, just because water is in coffee, that does not count!

Eat fresh and natural foods. Eating processed foods can wear your body down and keep you from being clean. Have you looked at those labels? Some of those words are longer than an address. Many processed foods can make you tired, worn out, and yucky. Much of the way you feel is based on what you eat; many don't realize or associate with this. So, eat foods that are clean, good, and balanced. You will feel the same.

There are numerous diets available. Try not to get wrapped up in a diet, but rather a way of life. Many doctors rave about the Mediterranean diet, which is based on a balanced approach to eating. The foods associated with this way of eating are vegetables, fruits, whole grains, beans, nuts, seeds, and olive oil. The focus on meats and proteins is on fish, poultry, beans, and eggs. The intake of red meat is minimal, and dairy products are consumed in moderation.

Choose a good food lifestyle. Do what is best for you. You can choose a known food plan or create your own. Just keep it clean and fill your body with good stuff.

Exercise. Another item on the list you often hear but want to ignore. Who has time? Or the energy? It was discussed earlier, and since you will be removing some things from your calendar, you can fit in exercise. Besides being great for your outer body, it is also fabulous for your emotional well-being. People who exercise feel better about themselves, feel less stress, and have a good outlook on life. It also makes you feel more in control during difficult situations. Exercise can be a great time to clear your mind, reduce stress, get away from the outside hustle and bustle, and focus on yourself.

This does not have to be a hardcore gym session. It can be a walk around the block with your dog. You don't have to pump a bar loaded with weights; you can use an exercise band instead. You don't have to be into CrossFit; a yoga session on a mat at home is a viable alternative. It doesn't have to be an hour; fifteen minutes is sufficient. You don't have to go to a gym. There are many free programs online. You don't have any excuses.

Any form of exercise is better than none. It makes you feel good, so why not add that to your schedule? If you don't use it, you lose it. Use it. Feel good. Feed your endorphins. Be good to your body. And do it without making excuses!

Meditate. People often think this is hard, but it can be made easier. The time you spend during meditation calms the body, mind, and spirit, bringing you closer to yourself and your awareness. You don't have to be religious to do this. It is a personal spiritual thing, not a religious thing. It is good for you and for cleaning your inner self. All you need to do is take ten to fifteen minutes to sit (or lie) comfortably, close your eyes, and breathe.

You can sit in a chair, cross-legged on the floor, or lie down during meditation. Do what is more comfortable for you and where you can relax your body. If sitting, place your hands on your knees with palms facing up. You can touch your thumb and index finger together on each hand. If lying down, your palms are facing up, and your hands are at your sides. Adjust your body so that you are elongated in your torso and your body is relaxed. Close your eyes—inhale with your belly, not your chest. Feel your stomach expand with the inhale, then feel it return with the exhale. Take a few deep breaths to help release any tension. With each exhale, feel the tension being released with it.

Turn on some relaxing music if you cannot focus in silence. Don't turn on a radio that plays commercials or has people talking. You can find apps on your phone that include spa or meditation music. Your primary focus is breathing and acknowledging each inhale and exhale. Do not let your mind wander about your daily activities, tomorrow's schedule, what to make for dinner, or the homework the kids will have. This is *your* time. It is time to find calm and recharge.

You can use mantras. If you are unsure what mantra to use, you can look some up online to assist you. You can make it simple: inhale positive and exhale negative. For example, if you are stressed about something coming up, you might say inside your head that *Everything will work out fine* during the inhale. During your exhale, you could say, *I release all stress.* Acknowledge that whatever happens is based on a larger plan and will work out as it should. Another example may be to say in your head during the inhale; *I am strong, confident, and successful.* During the exhale, *I release all fear, trying to stop me.* Fill yourself with positive energy and release all negative energy. Repeating this over with each breath calms the spirit and clears the mind to focus within.

If you are religious, your meditation time can be a spiritual experience through prayer. Do not use this as an opportunity to pray for all the world's problems or for everyone you know; you can pray for that later. This is a prayer time for you, something you may not be accustomed to since you usually pray for others. Use this time to pray and ask God to be with you, letting Him guide you on this journey. Ask Him to keep you strong and not to be discouraged. In times of decision-making, ask that He direct a path that is better for your well-being. And remind yourself, *'I can do all things through Christ who strengthens me.'* Meditate in a way that works best for you and allows your mind to be positive, focused, and in the moment. At the end of your meditation, take a few deep breaths, lie or sit for another few minutes, and slowly open your eyes to return to the present.

The time you spend on meditation is small compared to its benefits. Meditation helps calm anxieties, release stress, foster self-awareness, and aid in healing and improved sleep. There are many medical and spiritual benefits to meditation. It is a beautiful practice to add to your routine. If you want to eliminate negative energy from your body, this is a great way to achieve that.

Treat yourself. Bringing in the positive means feeding yourself with positivity. You can't keep putting it out without bringing something in. It would be best to treat yourself now and then to something special. It doesn't have to be massive or costly. It can be taking the time to walk around a lovely park, or sit on a bench and enjoy your surroundings, drinking a hot drink in the cold or a cold drink in the heat. Maybe you want to go to a play with a friend, have a dinner date with your spouse or significant other, get a new hairstyle, buy a new outfit, or do anything your little heart desires to feed your soul. Don't overdo it with a shopping spree or go to extremes. It's a treat. Just something small as a *'pick me up.'* But this little treat makes for enormous pleasure.

It would be nice to treat yourself weekly or biweekly. But remember, a treat is just that - a treat. Don't overindulge, and don't wait too long. Regular treats are needed because you deserve them.

Get outdoors. This does not mean walking out to the mailbox or driving to work and back. It means to get outdoors. Get some breaths of fresh air. Depending on where you live, enter the forest or go by the water. Some people are not outdoorsy, but fresh air, sun, and feeling the raw ground under your feet can make you feel better. Even a local park would be good. There are many paved trails you can ride a bike or walk on. Find some sand or water to sink your feet in. Being in the outdoors can relax you and relieve stress. It brings you to the moment. If you have outdoor anxiety, maybe open the windows in your house and let some fresh air waft through. Sit by the window and feel the breeze while breathing the fresh air. Do get outside in some way that takes you away from the daily grind. It is uplifting and brings goodness into your life. Being outdoors has many benefits, so fit this into your schedule as much as possible.

Do what you enjoy or work on your hobbies. Do not limit yourself to your daily normal functions of getting through life. You must do your work, chores, and whatever else you have, but don't let that be your life. Do things you enjoy. If you like hiking, get on those trails. If you like kayaking, get out in the water. If you like painting, get those brushes on canvas. If you enjoy collecting objects, go out looking for that particular item. If you like taking pictures, get out and snap those great shots. Don't put off doing what you enjoy. Many people do put that stuff off because there are more important things at hand. Yes, keep up with your daily responsibilities, but take time to enjoy what your heart desires. Those are just as important as your other essential things to do.

There will always be life to do. Doing what is important to you is life, too. Fit this in. Far too many people put off what they want and enjoy doing to keep other people's needs and joys met. Do not do this. Feed your wants and joys. If it's only a couple of hours a week, take it. Don't let that time get away from you.

Lastly, *mindfulness.* This is getting a little deep here, so let's keep it simple. Stay in the moment. Be conscious of who you are and what you are aiming for. Be mindful of your actions, and don't let others waste your time. Don't look ahead, and don't look back. Look at where you are right now and what you are trying to accomplish at this moment. Be aware of the changes you are making to better your world. Know you are worthy of these changes. You deserve to please your own life instead of everybody else's. You are allowed to say no if it doesn't work for *you*. You are allowed to say yes to anything that serves you well. Sometimes, you will need to go out of the zone and do things you don't care to do for the sake of others, but you now know your limits and you will not be stretched thin or beyond what is good for you. Exceptions happen, but you will not stay there. Stay focused.

If you're stressed or anxious about too much going on or having to say no to something you don't want or don't have time to do, stop! Before you overload your mind with worry, fret, and anxiety, take a moment and breathe. Take a few deep breaths and relax. Be present in the moment where you are, and don't get ahead of yourself. Don't think of all the negatives surrounding the moment. If you can, take a brisk walk to clear and sort your thoughts. If you can't get out, take some breaths and focus on the inhale and the exhale. Calm your inner self and be mindful of where you are and what you're feeling. Allow yourself to feel it, then let it go. Know that you will make the right decisions for you and your life. Let everything go and be just where you are. This is the only place you can be, so just be.

The *nice girl* is always out to please everyone and make them happy. It is now time to please yourself and make yourself happy. Clean out all the negative, toxic, and unneeded clutter (including people) in your life, and enjoy the lighter load with more space to fill with what is good for you.

Chapter Seven

Claim Who You Are

When I let go of what I am, I become what I might be.

~Lao Tzu

Let go of who you think people want you to be and be who you are. Do not try to be for everyone. Just be you. Our society tends to see people as their job. When meeting new people, one of the first questions is, "So what do you do?" They seem to rate them in their minds from that point on. It is only natural that many people define themselves by what they *do* and not by who they *are*. But you are you. You are your unique self. Sure, you may be a teacher, a drummer, a lawyer, or a soccer player, but that is what you do, not who you are as a person. You limit yourself when you define yourself as something you do. When you define yourself as who you are, you are limitless.

You have been a busy person, taking care of everyone and everything. You have been the *nice girl* for so long that you aren't sure who you are or what your true identity is. In the past, you have been the room mom, the PTA president, the scorekeeper, the house organizer, cook, family taxi, tutor, nurse, plus any outside job title that can describe who you are. The automatic response when someone asks what you do is your outside job title, but in your mind, you are screaming *everything!*

So, who are you? Don't automatically title yourself with your job title or what you do. Who are *you?* You are your given name. The name you were born with (or currently use). That is your identifier. Who is *that* person? Who are you on the inside? Think about that. When you go to a memorial service of someone who has passed, you don't hear, "Here lies the lawyer who was known well only for doing a good job at winning cases." And that's it. No, that is not how people are described or how you remember them. So why would you do that to yourself? At a memorial service, you usually hear, "Here lies John. A terrific man, brother, son, husband, friend, and dad. He was a wonderful person who would do anything for you. He was a role model to his community by supporting the Kids' Club. He was also a terrific attorney who won many cases, making the streets safer for us to be on," and so on. So, again, who are *you?*

Author's note: I was working with a client, and one problem that often came up during our sessions was self-discovery. She was having a hard time discovering who she was. She knew she was a mom, a wife, a grandma, a caregiver for her family, and a person who cared deeply for others. Her life consisted of house chores, watching kids, feeding animals, caring for the home, and not much else. She lost insight into who *she* was. She was doing something daily for everyone else but herself. She didn't have much self-worth because she didn't have a self-identity. She was so many things, but she felt like nothing. This is very common with the *nice girl*. They get lost in everything for everyone and forget who they are – *end author's note*.

With all of these changes you are making, this is the best time to claim your identity. Claim who you are as a person. Not the wife, mother, room mom, or PTA president, but the person. Who you *are*! You are the strong, caring, giving, loving, energetic, and inspiring person you are. You are not a title. You are so many adjectives rolled into a beautiful human being.

Many people prefer not to do work while reading books, but sometimes it's needed. Please get a pen and paper. Yes, that's right, a pen and paper. These items are not used much nowadays, as everything seems to be done on devices. However, handwritten notes can sometimes be better. Write down everything that you are. Describe yourself with adjectives and not nouns. It might take some time to think about it, but do take that time. Look inside yourself to see who you truly are.

Once you have written who you are, read that list a few times. This is how you see yourself. This is you as a person. Is this the person you want to claim? Is this the person you want to be? Is there something you want to remove or add? You can. But for right now, claim this person the way you are. This person is right here. Not a person for everyone else, but this person for you.

You need to understand that this *is* who you are. Claim it. Be it. Acknowledge it. This is the first time in a while that you are looking at yourself as a unique human who is not for everyone else but yourself. This is how you should be—YOU!

Now that you know who you are, be that person. Be the person you wrote down. You can stay that way or modify who you are. If you were to describe yourself in your written response as nouns, you would be the room mom, office manager, musician, dentist, etc. How can you elaborate on those? You can add job duties, but that still makes you a thing and not a being. By describing yourself with adjectives such as creative, ambitious, caring, thoughtful, etc., you create who you are—a particular kind of unique individual. Many people share the same adjective descriptors, but how you use them in your life makes you the unique person you are.

Do not let others claim you as theirs. Do not let the baseball coach claim you as the only one to keep score and plan the schedules. Do not let the PTA president claim you to be the fundraising organizer yearly and then add other duties. Do not let your friends claim you as the person who always puts on parties at your house and allows you to do all the heavy work. Do not let your family members claim you as the person who always goes to see them and does the driving. Claim you as the person you are, without others claiming you based on the giving and caring adjectives that describe you. Let them claim you for who you are, not what you can do for them.

You need to claim who you are and who you want to be. It is time to claim yourself as someone with dreams, goals, and ambitions. Allow yourself to be this person. Start working on becoming who you are and reaching farther to fulfill your own life's wants and needs, rather than those of others.

When you claim who you are, you are not isolating yourself from others or no longer helping out. You are not entirely quitting on volunteering or giving up your time. You are still going to assist in the areas you want. You are still going to care and be there when needed. The difference is that now it will be on *your* terms. It will be when you can, want, and need to. You will do what you want, but in the time frame you want to do it. You will no longer be driving yourself into the ground to please others. You will no longer have long nights working on many projects to keep everything going. You will no longer be worn ragged with too much on your plate. You will no longer be hurting yourself while trying to please everyone but you. You will no longer be silent or have your time abused so others can play.

It is time to do what you want to do when you want to do it, and nothing more than that. It is time to work on your dreams and goals. It is time to work on self-care and give time to your life that has been lacking. Many times, you do what others want you to do. Many times, you do what life brings to you. Many times, you do it for convenience. It is hard to step outside of the box and do what is wanted for ourselves. This is your time to step outside of that box and do what is right for you. Claim your dreams and goals. Accept them, and don't let them sit and wait any longer. Take this time to be you and follow where you want to go with your life.

Claiming who you are now does not detract from what you have been. It enhances you. It brings more to your life. A nice person can still be nice and help out when it is convenient for her. Just because you are making changes and doing what you want in your life, you can still take the time and keep your foot in the door, but just a foot. Don't throw your whole self in there again unless it is for you to fulfill your actual wants and needs.

Author's note: I will give you an example of claiming who you are. I have wanted to write a book since I was in the sixth grade. I always wanted to help people, too. I loved reading Dear Abby's advice column and wanted to have my own column. I also wanted to be a psychiatrist, but then I wanted to be a nurse. With all of those wants, I went for the nurse plan. I was going to apply to a college to become a nurse in another state, but I started dating someone. Instead, I stayed in town and applied for night school in accounting—a far cry from becoming a nurse. I didn't want to move away from this relationship, and nursing would be crazy hours that I thought wouldn't work well for us. Accounting would be a good job, and I would be home at regular hours.

I ended up getting married and having a child. I also did not finish the accounting courses because the college wasn't accredited and shut down. I had traded one goal for another, which is what we sometimes do in our lives, and that is okay, but in my heart, I didn't do it for the right reasons, and didn't even try with my original goal. It was a self-inflicted change to please someone else. It was a mess, and I still had to pay for the time I went to college even though I had no degree. I had no degree in nursing, accounting, or anything. I was so upset that I didn't follow my first path to nursing school. I chose a path I thought was best for someone else and wanted to make everyone happy, but it didn't do well for anyone. Most importantly, I wasn't happy. It took some time, but I finally found a place in my life that led me to other things I appreciate. I look back now, and I know that if I had followed that nursing path, then I wouldn't have had my son, and I wouldn't have been led to where I am now, with two beautiful daughters.

I was living a life for others and keeping it convenient and sustainable. I still yearned to help people and write, but I kept putting my dreams aside. I was living life and enjoying the journey, but I always felt something was missing. I wasn't living for me! I was living how I thought others felt I *should* be.

Time has gone on. It has been about twenty-seven years from that point of changing out my nursing dream to when I decided to claim who I really was. It was time to claim the person I wanted to be. It is time to claim the helper, creative, caring, loving, and ambitious person I am. The person who will make me an author. The column writer. The advice giver. The artist. It was time! I had a detour that took much longer than I planned, but I claimed her! That is how our journeys work. We have to live a little, get tired a little, get down a little, get inspired a little, step up a little, and then it is time. It can happen in a few months, a few years, or, in my case, many years. I could only write what I do now with my life experiences. I need to be authentic about what I write. I would rather have waited to do it right than to push it and have done it wrong – *end of author's note*.

Now is your time. Now is the time to claim who you are. By knowing who you are, you can do things you have wanted to do or be. Turn your nouns into adjectives and your adjectives into nouns. You can turn a busy, scattered woman into an adventurous, spontaneous one. Or a tired, overworked nurse into a motivational, energetic life coach. A disrespected, underpaid classroom teacher becomes a vibrant, inspiring online teacher. These are just examples and not insinuating that you have to change your outside job or do something drastic. You can still lead the life you live, but know who you are. Feel more in tune with yourself and what you want and need out of life. Lightening your load a little will give you new insight into what is important to you. Knowing who you are can make you that much more authentic.

You can use this time just to be. Be the mom you have wanted to be. Be the employee you have wanted to be. Be the artist you have wanted to be. Be the wife you have been wanting to be. Be the friend you have been wanting to be. Be the golfer you want to be. You can take unnecessary busy off your plate and focus on being the fun, thoughtful, inspiring, caring, loving, adventurous, and focused mom you want to be. Or stop taking on so many projects at work and focus on your primary duties. You don't need to excel so much at your job that it takes away from other parts of your life. Prove to yourself that you can be balanced. You can work hard and be excellent at your job while being committed to your other activities, relationships, or wants in life.

Claim that person and be her. Don't let other outside sources take you away from being who you are and want to be. You now know how to say yes to what is suitable for you. You know where your priorities lie. You know what makes you who you are and how you want to live. Claim it.

This is a time for you to re-evaluate relationships. Are they working for you? Are they making you feel good about who you are? Are they supporting your changes or trying to suck you back into what works for them? Suppose you want to be outgoing, spontaneous, vibrant, and free-flowing, and a family member, friend, or lover makes you feel unworthy of anything you want to be, or fights these changes you are making. In that case, consider if the relationship is positive for you. You don't have to end it entirely, but you may want to step back or set boundaries for what you will tolerate. You sacrifice for those you love, but you will no longer lose yourself. You should be able to be loved for who you are and supported for what you want to do. You are making massive progress and don't need to be pulled back or down. If it is negative, let it go.

You have to know that this is *your* life. No one is living it for you, and you can't live it for others. You will give and take. You will have hardships. You will let go of something and relationships, and work to save others. You know how they will affect your well-being. Is the lady torturing you to be on the PTA board someone to sacrifice for? No. Is getting up at five o'clock in the morning to exercise before your day starts getting busy worth your sacrifice? Of course. You need to pick your sacrifices and know your worth.

People might start to see your changes at this point and wonder what is going on with you. That is a good thing. Just let them keep wondering. If you want to share your journey with others, that is entirely up to you. Sometimes, it is best to keep on the path and move on alone until you want others to join in. Some people will not understand or care. Some will still make it about them. You keep doing you. You are not being rude, selfish, or mean. You are being true to yourself, and it has been long overdue. Claim her!

Chapter Eight

It's All About You

If you don't design your own life plan, chances are, you'll fall into someone else's.

~Anonymous

Look at how far you have come! Isn't this great? A new way of living. A new you! Not because anything has been wrong, but because everyone can use some changes now and then to enhance their life. As discussed in the last chapter, it's time to let go of who you think people want you to be and just be who you are.

It is your life. Now that you have claimed what you want to do and what you want to be, create it! Create the life you want to live. It is all about you. It is about what you want to see, what you want to wear, where you want to go, and how you spend your time—saying *yes* to what makes you happy. Saying *yes* to what gives you positive energy. Saying *yes* to what will make you grow as a person. Saying *yes* to what makes you feel good!

In reality, it won't seem like much will change. You will still be who you are, doing the job you have been working, making dinner when you get home, running the same basic errands, and living your daily life. It won't be some dramatic one-eighty in a new house, with a new family, with a powerhouse job. BAM! There it is! Nope, it won't be like that. Your changes will be as gradual as you want and at a pace that works for you. It may take some time before you notice the progress you have made. People you are around or in contact with may never notice these changes. The people using you and your skills will notice once you remove yourself from them and into your new lifestyle. There may be people you spend more time with who will notice you are more present than before. And even then, some of them won't pay attention. The only person fully aware of any of this is you! And that is okay because it is all about you anyway.

You have decided to say yes only to positive things for yourself. You are eliminating wasted time and exertion on non-meaningful areas of your life. You are removing yourself from many tasks that others can handle without you. This will allow you more time for yourself and the goals you want to work on achieving. So, focus on going even deeper. Why not? You are already this far.

How is your attitude? This is important. Are you still all in with this? Are you still focused and excited about the changes and where they can lead you? Or are you doubting yourself and what may lie ahead? Your attitude will determine where you go with this, how far you will help yourself, and how much effort needs to be placed. These changes are only as good as you make them. You can often be excited to start something and feel all gung-ho, but before you're halfway through, you may already be done and want it over. This could be like trying a new diet program or painting a room in your house. Sometimes, you must push through, focus on the outcome, and remind yourself how all this effort will be worth it. You wouldn't want to paint only half of a room and quit, and you don't want to quit on this effort halfway through, either.

Keep your attitude in check. Keep your spirits up. Sometimes, it might bring you down, or you don't see the positive outcome of your changes. Ignore that. Whenever something is worth it, you may get thoughts that will try to keep you from the reward. Don't let this happen. Remind yourself how important you are to focus on. Remind yourself that just because you no longer want to be the *nice girl* doesn't make you a bad girl for wanting to do what is right for you. Remind yourself that people who have succeeded with a considerable accomplishment may have fallen over a hundred times before reaching it. Remind yourself that you only have one life to live, and you must live the best life for *you* now. There are a hundred reasons not to put your best effort into this, but there is one huge reason you should: you! Keep positive and keep pushing!

This is also a great time to reflect. Are you happy with the specific changes you are making now? Are there more you want to try? Are you where you want to be? Are there goals you still want to accomplish that you didn't list? Where is your focus going to go from here?

Those thoughts may help you better understand what has been missing in your life while you were busy pleasing everyone else. Where do you want to go from here? You have already thought of this, or you wouldn't be making changes. But have you reflected on them? You can be so busy that your thoughts swarm in your head, jumbled with those of others. You think about errands, meetings, dates, *why do I stay in this relationship*, events, *I need to exercise, why can I not just tell her no, where did I put that stapler, I need to find a new job*, dry cleaning, *I am having a bad hair day*, pedicure, *I really cannot keep doing this with the PTA, what do I make for dinner tonight, I am so tired of being everyone's doormat.* You thought of it, but did you *really* think of it?

While in this process, take the time to see how you got to where you are and what you need to do to move on to the next phase. There are suggestions in this book for changes that may need to be made, but you are the only one living your life, and you know exactly what needs to be done for yourself. You are the only one who knows where things need to stop and where new life needs to begin. This is your story. Reflect on that. Reflect on yourself. Not on what the world sees or should see, but what you need and where you want to be.

After your reflection, this is a beautiful time to focus on the next step. With all the changes you have made and are still planning to make, you may still wonder where you are going from here. What is the big plan? What should this all lead to? One of the best ways to do this is by making a plan. You can make it in years. Choose a 1, 5, or 10-year plan. You can also do it by month, school quarters, work contracts, or whatever suits your needs. Don't just make this plan in your head. Write it down. Put it on paper. Typing it out will be a good way, too. Just as long as it is put somewhere into words so you can read it, keep it, and use it.

Put some thought into this. Don't be vague and write down, *in one year, I want to lose 20 pounds and sell handmade crafts.* This is a plan. It would be best to write it down in steps and dates to evaluate where you are and how much further you should go. For example, what must you do to make this happen if you want to lose twenty pounds in a year? You could list how many days and the time you will need to exercise each week. What foods do you want to eliminate from your diet? What foods or drinks should you add to your diet, such as green tea and/or vegetables? Are you a stress eater, bored eater, or don't have portion control? Think about changing your plate size and eliminating second helpings. Drink water when you get the urge to snack. Eat a piece of dark chocolate when you get a sweet craving. Write down your plan for accomplishing the goal, and do not just write down the goal itself. Your body and mind control what you will do, but writing out your plan gives it power and existence.

If you want to sell your craft items, what do you need for this? You may want to invest in a portable table to sell at craft fairs, farmers' markets, and local events. Do you have a website or a social media page to advertise your products? Do you have a specific population you are trying to sell to? There are also online markets where you can place your items. Keep items in your car in case anyone asks about them. Pass out business cards. It's all about the plan and the journey. Both are just as important to keep you on track and get you to that destination.

With the plans being made and steps being checked off, sometimes plans change. Things may happen in life that can derail you. That is okay. Do not get hugely discouraged and give up. If this one specific plan does not come to pass, change your plan. For instance, if you have been trying to lose weight with your plan, but your scale is not budging, change the goal. How are you feeling? How is your energy? How is your muscle tone? Maybe it is not just weight you want to lose, but now you want to be healthier. It is not just about the scale but your stamina. Is working out helping you to have more energy to get your tasks done throughout the day? Are your clothes fitting better with your body toning up? Does your health feel better when you eat cleaner foods and drink more water? Of course, you want extra pounds to drop, but look at the larger view: what you are accomplishing and what else you can achieve. Keep your mind open to more, and allow yourself to live more fully.

It is still your plan, even if the original one didn't work out as you wanted. Plans can be adjusted. You can make a new one or add to existing ones. You are not limited to specific thoughts, goals, and dreams. Sometimes, the changed plan even turns out to be better. You don't have time for discouragement here. It is still all about you. Keep that focus, that 'push through' attitude, and make it all work out for the best. Remember, these are plans. It is a guide, not a permanent contract. You will use them to help you reach your goals in life and what you want to accomplish, but plans can change. If that happens, then you change to a new plan. Don't make it devastating. It's just an inconvenience. Maybe it is a vast inconvenience, but it is nothing you can't get around. Enjoy the journey. It isn't always about reaching the final destination. The lessons on the way to it are your growth.

Get inspired. Something triggered you to make changes in your life. It could have been exhaustion, certain voids, being so busy but not fulfilled, caving to others but not yourself, or something else. Did something inspire you? Did you see another person act so blissfully self-confident and caring for her own needs that you felt the need to do the same? Did you think of an epiphany where you saw yourself in a different life that suddenly inspired your change? After that burst of inspiration, now what?

Maybe you know the changes you want, and this book is helping you to make them, but it is still difficult to see the long term. Or you are concerned you will lose focus. Life will get in the way, and you will lose sight of the bigger picture. You could make a vision/goal board that you can see daily. Put images and quotes to motivate and inspire you to continue this journey. If you want more time for fabulous getaways, put pictures of scenic beaches or forests with waterfalls. If you're going to start taking care of yourself more with self-pampering, put pictures of spas and massages. If you want a better career, put pictures of an office with the corner window, speaking in front of the crowd, or maybe flying for meetings. Whatever you want for your plan, put those visions before you to inspire you to get there. Don't just look at your board, but visualize it in your head as if you are there.

You can also research how others may have accomplished similar plans. Everything is online nowadays. You can find a blog, a video, or an article on almost anything your heart desires. Find inspiration from others who have done it before you and get some basics that can lead the way in something new. Use the tools that are out there. Although you will be getting information from someone else, it does not lessen the importance of the changes it makes for you. It is still about you. It will *always* be about you.

Another way to stay inspired is to journal. Some people may opt for journaling instead of creating a vision board, while others may do both. Choose whatever helps you reach your goals. Journaling is a great way to record your thoughts, plans, and actions, bringing them to life, creating more accountability, and strengthening self-discipline.

Writing it out can give you a better perspective of what you are setting out to accomplish. It can be an excellent tool to help you see your progress when you feel like nothing is being done. It can also allow you to release your fears and anxieties while finding strength and determination to continue. Bringing your feelings out on paper can be beneficial to your progress. While writing about your daily plan, goals, steps you are taking, and accomplishments, you can also write down any frustrations, delays, problems, or concerns you might have. By writing them down, you release them. Write them down, feel them, and then let them go. This is also a great time to write down what you did for yourself that day, how much better you are feeling since making choices that benefit your life, the strength you had that day, *not* saying yes or no, and living in a way that is positive for you. Take this in and give yourself credit for the good that you are doing for you!

We mostly keep thoughts in our heads and figure it out from there. This approach works for many people, but if you're a visual person, consider keeping a journal to track your plans, goals, daily progress, and maintain accountability to stay focused. This could be an asset for you. Again, this is about you and your life; do what works best for you while making the right changes. For so long, it has been about other people, and you may slip off course and fall into old habits. Having a vision board and/or journaling can be a fabulous way to keep you focused while working on yourself and your goals.

Many times, the *nice girl* is seeking validation from the outside world. Now, it is time to validate yourself. You can do this! You do not need other people to encourage you. You will be your best encourager. You know how important you are. Your time, well-being, goals, and daily life are the primary focus right now. Of course, you are not pushing everyone else out, but you are limiting what you give them while paying more attention to *your* needs and wants. This means focusing on yourself without others' approval, encouragement, or guidance. If you get the approval, encouragement, or guidance, that is a huge bonus that you can use, but don't expect it.

As you continue this journey, you will learn about yourself and what you want from life. You will become aware of what you no longer accept and what you want to bring into your life. You will discover your true positive friends and family, as well as those with whom you must end ties. You will continue to do activities that enhance you, but stop any that no longer serve you. It is all about prioritizing your needs. What suits you, and what steps must you take to move in a better direction? You may make mistakes, change your mind a few times, and go past your limitations, and that is alright. Sometimes, you need to figure out things by trial and error. Just learn from the experience, brush it off, and keep going.

Acknowledge your emotions, strengths, courage, determination, and success. This is very important. Every effort you put in deserves your attention. Take a moment to say something good about yourself and let yourself know how proud you are of your progress. Don't condemn yourself if you falter; instead, be your own encourager and keep pushing forward - not just with the changes you're making, but with life itself. This includes aspects such as your job, exercise routine, family meals, and significant decisions in the future. Be aware of your steps, encourage yourself, and praise yourself as you go. If you falter, acknowledge that, learn from it, and keep pushing through. You deserve every bit of recognition for your efforts and progress.

Since it's all about you, have fun! This would be a great time to treat yourself to a few new clothes if they are within your budget. Feeling new and fresh can help give you the boost you need to stay focused. Something about a new shirt or pair of jeans makes you feel good. Nothing too bold, or why not? Go for the gusto. It's often mentioned that you should do things for yourself because you need reminders that it is okay to do things for yourself.

All those times you felt guilty when buying a new pair of shoes or getting a dress for a special occasion, and thought that money should go to the kids' school projects or your spouse's new golf clubs, guilt no more. Since everyone is being taken care of, everyone includes you, too. It is best that you are taken care of and get the things that you want and need. Do you feel guilty when you buy your kids new school clothes? Do you feel guilty when you buy something special for your husband? Do you feel guilty buying a special gift for a great friend? Do you feel guilty when purchasing the perfect presents for family members? You most likely don't, so do not feel guilty when buying something special for yourself. You deserve it! Treating yourself well is a way of valuing and appreciating yourself, and it is necessary.

When it is said that it is all about you, don't turn this into an excuse to be rude. That is not what this is about. You don't need the approval of others, but you still don't want to be insensitive either. This is about including yourself when it comes to some pampering—not feeling guilty when you buy something special for yourself—doing things that are positive for your soul—doing things that you want to and not for any other reason. Say *yes* to volunteering your time if it will make you happy and benefit you while helping others, but do not let it deplete you. Also, don't do anything that is for seeking acceptance or out of fear. Afraid you won't be accepted or included in the future. Afraid you won't be essential. You are!

Remove toxic, energy-draining people from your life and replace them with fun and uplifting ones. Consider your feelings, and do not base your actions on how others will feel about your decision. You will know how to respond. Some people do what is right for themselves, but in a callous way. Do not be this person. You will no longer be a *nice girl,* but you still want to be kind. And because you have cared for so many people for so long, it may be challenging to prioritize yourself, and you might worry about what others think; that is okay. Your heart can change some things, but not everything. Just do your best to make decisions that are beneficial for *you.*

No one can do what is best for you except you. Others can assist in doing what may benefit you, but that is a temporary fix. You need to be the one who will make those decisions for the rest of your life. What a beautiful thing it is that you can control most of your happiness and well-being if you allow yourself to do so.

Chapter Nine

When They Say No

You have to say no to a lot of things in order to be able to say yes to a lot of great things ~ Unknown

How many times have others told you no? A few? A lot? Does it seem that while you are always saying yes to everyone else and willing to squeeze things in to get them all done, the one time you ask for anything, the answer is no? Are you being said no to so often that you don't ask anymore and do it all yourself? Many people say no to you, so why is it so difficult to say no to them?

You are a *nice girl* who doesn't want to upset anyone by saying no, but you allow and accept being told no. You will accept it because you want to please everyone and not ruffle feathers. You don't want their feelings to be hurt or put them in a difficult situation. It is always about pleasing them. And when they say no to you, you understand they are too busy to help. You know it is too far for them to drive.

You can relate to the fact that they are too tired. Not everyone can say yes; you get that, so if you need to say no, then others should understand, too.

You are the person who, when someone says no to you, will figure it out. You have been doing this for years. Accept it and move on. You don't end the friendship, relationship, business connection, or social group; you accept the *no* and keep moving forward. People have lives. They are busy, stressed, tired, and have other things going on, and that is just life. Or maybe they don't want to do it, plain and simple. So, it is a no. You might be upset but not devastated. You get through it. Life continues, and the people who said no keep living and moving on, too. But with you, you can't seem to get the word no out to others, regardless of how many times it has been said to you.

Many people go out of their way to help others. They are not trying to impress or get recognition, but just being nice. They are not the *nice girl.* They are people just living their lives and assisting if asked or needed. They don't fill up their schedules. They don't go all out to be the yes person. They don't forget to fulfill their own lives while helping others. They do it when they can, when they want to, and because it lifts their spirits when they do. They also know when and how to say no. You can say yes many times and be nice, but you are still allowed to say no when you can't or don't want to do something. You know some people who are so nice they will give you the shirt off their back, but will still say no when something doesn't work for them. They have even said no to you. But they are still very nice. You admire them. You envy how they can say no and not seem to shudder at their decision. You think it is wonderful how they balance their lives with so many yeses, but they will say no, too. You want to be this way. And you will. Now!

First of all, not everyone is a *nice girl.* They don't feel guilty about saying no and let it consume them, or overanalyze everything. They do what works for them. If they have time, they do it. If they can do a specific task, they will. If they don't know how to do something, they say no and let someone who knows how to do it. They won't say yes and then stress themselves out on how to get it done because they are afraid to say no. They won't fill their schedule so full that they get frazzled about how they will complete everything. They are not worried about impressing others with their yeses. And they are not concerned about upsetting others with their no's. They balance. It's not about fulfilling everyone else's needs but just living life and doing what they can, when they can.

Saying no to someone is hard. If you have been the yes person for a long time, people will not expect to hear no from you. It may be challenging to say and for others to hear. It could be uncomfortable, cause turmoil, and possibly end a relationship. This is something you have been avoiding for a long time. This is what you have been trying not to face. But saying yes when you don't want to can be worse. For your health, your well-being, and your livelihood. People move in and out of our lives. Your life is the one that will stick with you your entire lifetime. You need to do what is best for you. The others will continue for themselves.

Do you think it doesn't bother those people who say no? It probably does, but they don't dwell on it. You will learn to do this, too. You are not going to turn into a *no-person.* You will not say it all the time, just when you know it doesn't work for you or your goals. As you make these changes to better yourself, it will be essential to establish boundaries. This will be for groups, volunteer positions, work, and relationships. When you say no to something, it will let the other person know your expectations, what you have time for, what works for you, and what you are willing and not willing to do. You will say *yes* to things that work for you, better you, and lead you to reach your goals and enhance your life. But sometimes, the word *no* will need to be said.

Think of how others have said no to you. Were they rude or curt? Were they sympathetic and explanatory? Was it a matter of fact? Did it hurt you? Did you understand and move on? When you think of how others have said no to you, you will know how you want to say no to others. Some will not always be understanding when you say no to them. That is OK. You say it and move forward. Do not go back on it and cave in with a yes out of guilt. If you do that, you remove any boundaries that are trying to be set and allow people to use you whenever needed. Stick to your *no*! You don't know how to say no? The best way to say no is to say it. And be honest.

If you lie, you will feel the guilt and the anguish, and you will tear yourself apart. So, don't do that. Just say no and give a brief reason why. Brief! Don't go into a complete story and try to justify why you are saying no. That looks like you are trying to validate for yourself and not the other person. And they don't want to hear it. You already said no, so what comes after that is a blur to them. Be authentic and honest. *I am sorry, but I cannot do this right now. I have a busy schedule, and I really cannot fit in.* Or, *thank you so much for considering me, but I must decline at this time. Please keep me in mind for the future.* Maybe, *no, thank you. I already have plans, but I appreciate you asking.* Keep it simple. Give a brief explanation, but not a life story, on why you can't. When you do this and keep it open for the future, you can say yes if you can at that time.

There may be some you don't want to leave the future open to. You get stomach pains just thinking they will ask you again, and you will have to go through the whole process over and over. Be firm if someone asks you, and you want to ensure the boundary is set. Polite but firm. You may say something like, *Thank you for asking, but I am not interested in that.* Or *I appreciate you considering me, but I must decline now and in the future.* You may get someone determined to change your mind; do not let them. Stay focused on what is best for you. There are times you can or must bend. Your workplace would be one of them. You can take on so much, but when the boss asks or tells you to do a project, you often have to figure it out and add it to your plate. If it is a position where you can say something about it, then speak! Set that boundary.

When you say no to others, be consistent with your no. Make sure you follow through and continue in the future. You don't want to be wishy-washy. You also don't want to say no to one person and yes to someone else for the same thing or something similar. Don't make it more of a problem than it already is to you. Keep it simple.

It is okay to feel bad when saying *no.* Feeling bad is common. Dwelling on it, feeling guilty, and making yourself sick over it is *not* okay. Some people are concerned about the outcome of giving a *no* response: will the person get upset, will it cause a problem with the relationship, will it make them appear unreliable, or will it hurt future chances of being asked? Let those thoughts go.

Yes, some people may get upset about being told no. They need you for something that you will not provide. They will continue to ask others until they get a yes. If it causes a problem and they cannot understand your reasoning from your side, that is *their* problem. The *nice girl* is terrified of these outcomes. That is why she always says yes. However, you are now a nice person, not that *nice girl*. You have every right to set boundaries and only help when you want.

Many successful people say no. This is why they are successful. They don't waste their time on things that do not benefit them. They say yes to things that help them reach their goals and move them forward. They say yes to experiences that bring excitement and adventure into their lives. They say yes to people who can help them and who they can help in return. They say yes to anything that can make their lives feel more fulfilling. It is not selfish or rude. It is how they want their life to be. They consciously decide not to fill their days with non-fulfilling things or activities. They don't waste their time on meaningless tasks.

If you want to be successful in making positive changes in your life, you will need to say no to anything that does not serve you or that you do not want to do. You can say no if you are over-stressed and asked to be a scorekeeper for your kid's sports games. Don't have this in your head… *I am at the games anyway, so I might as well keep score while I am there.* No. Being at the game and keeping score differs from watching your kid play, socialize, and relax. Let someone else do it, and take that time to enjoy it. Don't add to your stress with more. It will be stressful to say no, but you will gain peace of mind soon after chatting and cheering in the stands. Maybe someone else wants to do it, but assumes it is always you. If it isn't fully working for you, say no. Someone else will appreciate keeping score.

How many times have friends said no to you? They can't make it. They have other plans. Sometimes, people cannot say yes. They have different priorities. It is okay. Why do you think your friends will not do the same for you? Why are you always saying yes, even when it doesn't work for you? Do you think your friends will not give you the same consideration? If they don't, are they really friends? How you treat your friends is how they should also treat you. If you need or want to say no, they should understand. They should accept that and know there will be a next time if needed.

Saying no is such a powerful act. You know this. As you say it more often, it will become easier to say. Staying true to yourself and what is right for you will be easier. You will find it easier to keep those boundaries. You will know what works for you and what doesn't. You will know when to say yes. You will find more self-discovery by saying no because you will learn what suits you. Saying no will be a positive. You will use this word when something is negative to you physically or emotionally.

This is a hard step to take, but a necessary one. Not everyone says yes *all* the time. Recall when you have been told no. Keep true to yourself, your goals, and your changes. Be a nice person and say no politely, with a brief explanation. Thank them for asking, and move on from it. Someone may get their feelings hurt, be disappointed, and maybe upset, but a genuine relationship will withstand a no now and then.

It was discussed earlier in the book when to say yes. You say yes when it is suitable for your goals, well-being, livelihood, and soul. So, before you say no, ask yourself if doing whatever is asked will benefit you. Will it better you? Will it make you feel good? Will it lift your spirits? If you said yes, then go ahead and do it. But if you answered no to any, their answer would be no. You get the point. It is okay to say no; people have said no to you.

Chapter Ten

Enjoy The Journey

You won't be happy at the destination if you can't be happy on the journey

~ Unknown

You have read this far and feel so great about the changes you have already made and will continue to make, but at some point, you may start to waver. You might think about how tough it will be to continue or what if you fail. What if you can't do it? What if you can't change or you revert? You could be getting negative thoughts in your head before you fully get on the journey. Don't do that!

Look at you. Really, look at you! Look in the mirror at that beautiful person looking back at you. Look into those eyes and see what is there. Are you feeling good about the changes you are making? Do you feel better letting some things go? Are you enjoying that you are now taking more care of yourself? Can you feel burdens lifting and your heart filling? Can you feel the excitement of new adventures coming your way? The answer to all of these should be yes.

As it has been said before, it will not happen overnight. Some of these changes will take time. You may be locked into an agreement or have obligations that must be fulfilled for a while. It may take time to search and land a new job. You may have to save money to move to a new neighborhood. You might have committed to a school year of activities. Just because you could have delays in some areas does not mean you cannot immediately make changes in others. Be proud of yourself for taking these steps to move in the direction of where you want to be.

If you are having some delays, look at them as building blocks to help you be better prepared for moving on from that area. If you jump the gun in some situations, it may complicate the change. So, ride it out and focus on what you can. Enjoy the whole journey, not just the destination. You will learn so much during this time. You will start understanding more about what you want and need. Take your time. You don't want to hurry and miss important things that will benefit you. But also, don't hold yourself back and take too much time, so that you are not making progress.

The journey will be inspiring for you. This is a time to discover your strengths and work on your weaknesses. Using the courage you didn't know you had and pushing through like a woman on a beautiful mission. Being a warrior in pursuit of happiness is a wonderful thing! So, enjoy it. You know parts of it won't be easy, and it might take a bit of time. You also know that change isn't always easy, but it is necessary. You know it is time. You know you are worth it. You know your energy is needed in other places. You know the *nice girl* has to leave now, and you can be a nice person with boundaries.

You might experience roadblocks. Do not quit. Just take a detour. You will have some family and friends supporting the changes, giving you a boost to carry on, but you will also have some who will battle you and try to hold you back. When the battle happens, you may want to fall into *nice girl* mode and do what you can to please them. You won't want to cause a commotion and, instead, give in to their wants. Don't!

You will need to remind yourself at those times whose life you are living. Are you living their life and doing what you can to make it better for them? Or are you living *your* life, your only life, doing what you must do for *yourself*? There will be challenging moments when you cannot say yes to someone, but that will benefit you. Just hold true to yourself. If, now and then, you want to say yes to something to avoid a vast conflict, do it and then move on from that. It doesn't mean you failed. You know what is best for you and are still moving forward with the changes. It is nice to help someone, but then move on and pursue what is true to you. Once in a while, it is okay. Sometimes, you will do things you don't necessarily want to do. This is not a setback, but do not make it a habit you are already trying to break. You need to stay on track. Do it and then move on.

Don't question everything. If something has been asked of you, don't question if you are giving in as a *nice girl* or saying yes as a nice person. Don't stress over that. You will know. If you feel like it is something you want to do and it will make you feel good, do it. If you are not really into it and it feels stressful or burdensome, don't. It really can be that simple if you let it be. The *nice girl* is so pleasing and doing things out of concern for what others are thinking or how they will react. A nice person is doing something they want to do because it will make them feel good while helping another. It might get mixed at first, but after a bit (and you probably already know it, but don't admit it to yourself), your decisions on your actions will be strictly based on your best interest. Stay true to you! You have your best life to take action on. Continue on this path. There is so much ahead waiting for you to explore. Enjoy and know that what is coming will be wonderful and positive. This moment is wonderful and positive. You have already begun!

Do not second-guess yourself or feel guilty for doing things for yourself. Don't sit there and think, *'I shouldn't be doing this. I shouldn't be buying something for myself like this. This is so selfish.'* No, it is not! Selfish people are those who use you because they know you won't say no. Selfish people are the ones making you feel less than if you don't do what is best for them. Selfish people are those who don't consider your feelings when you are tired, worn, and self-deprived while you continue to help them out. It is not selfish to live a life that is good for you, especially your physical and mental self. Putting yourself first when you have been putting everyone else before you is not selfish. Loving yourself enough to feed your soul positive energy is not selfish. Buying something for yourself that you want or need is not selfish. Selfishness is having a disregard for others and being concerned exclusively with oneself.

The problem with the *nice girl* is that she often prioritizes the needs of others over her own. Adding yourself into the mix of people you are pleasing is not selfish one bit. It is necessary and will help you thrive more in your own life. There is nothing selfish about that. So, lose that guilt and go out there, make decisions, and take actions that suit your new lifestyle. You need to enjoy this time fully, not question it.

Once you are in the flow of your changes, it will become your lifestyle. It will become natural and less emotionally confusing to make decisions. The entire process is your personal journey, and the outcome will depend on how you navigate it. You might fall back twenty times and feel like giving up, but don't! You keep pushing through and know that tomorrow is another day. Some of the best things in your life are the hardest to achieve, but they are very well worth it. Do not give up! Your best life depends on it.

For some, the changes may come more quickly, while others struggle or take more time. It is not a race; it is a journey. Take in every moment along the way. You have been waiting too long to say yes to yourself and limiting yourself while pleasing others. This was just the opportune time, so you took it and ran with it. Good for you. You keep running and enjoy that runner's high. Not the race, but rather the run. Someday, it will slow down, and you will be right where you need to be. You can then walk it out. But what a great adrenaline rush to come down from, right? Breaking free and knowing that each step is filled with power and strength is worth it, just like running a marathon. It is about putting all your effort, hard work, heart, and soul into it so you can have that fabulous feeling of crossing the finish line. Then, you relax, enjoy your accomplishments, and return to your daily workout routine to keep your body in shape for the next race.

These changes will be similar to a marathon. You work out and prepare your body for the long haul of that run. You make some adjustments to your routine and push harder because you need to ensure you are doing what is best for you so that you can finish. You will focus on your eating, workout routines, rest, and breathing to ensure you are in the best shape to run across that finish line. Then you run. You pace yourself so you won't burn out early and can keep a pace that keeps you moving the entire time. There may be moments when you don't feel like you are in the best shape for this, and it is getting too tough. You might think several times that you want to quit. It is too hard, and you didn't know it would be so difficult. You keep running and gasping for air. You are sweating and wondering if this is worth it.

Did you do the right things to prepare? Are the changes you made with diet and workouts the right ones for you to get through this? You think of the people who thought you were crazy to put yourself through all that and push yourself so hard. Were they right? But then you see the finish line. It is right ahead of you. You are wearing down. You are struggling to get there. Do you just quit now, even though you are so close? You drag those feet with every step. Almost there. Do not give up now. Do not quit! You cross the finish line. You did it. You pushed through, and you didn't stop. It was all worth it. You accomplished your goal!

After the marathon, the runner takes a little rest but continues to work out to keep their body in shape. They continue to make good choices that will benefit their bodies and keep them in prime condition. You will make choices that will continue to be good for you. These choices will bring change that will keep you at your best life, living deeply and doing what is right for you. These choices will prepare you for the next run that may come your way. When you struggle to do what is best for you and not someone else, you will be better prepared to make the right choices for you and not give up or give in. You will reach your goals!

You may have some difficult moments. You might sweat with fear or anxiety, but you will keep going. You may get tested to see if you have enough strength to get through it. Did you let go of the right things? Are you making good choices? Did you eliminate enough? Can you keep this up? It will all swirl in your head. You will question yourself and your worthiness. You will doubt your ability to push through. But you will keep pushing. You may struggle at times. But you will push on, and you will make it!

You have made choices to rid your daily life of negative, toxic, and mentally exhausting elements. You will now only say yes to what you want and what benefits you. Now you rest a bit. Then, you will keep a daily routine just like the runner. The runner must consistently feed their body with good food and workouts daily to stay in good shape. You must continue to make good choices and feed your soul positive energy to keep on the right course.

Enjoy the journey because these changes will give you a favorable outcome. This is how your journey *should* be. You may not like the fact that you will not say yes to specific situations, but you know it will benefit you not to. You may have difficulty taking care of yourself, but you know it will benefit you now and in the future. So, enjoy this.

Enjoy every bit of change, struggle, victory, and this time of your life.

This is very exciting. It can be scary, uncertain, and challenging, but still very exciting. Take it all in. Embrace it. This could be where you often want to reach the destination and get it over with. Get through all the complex parts and live your simpler life of not feeling so overwhelmed by everyone using your niceness. It would be good, but then you wouldn't take these changes in. They might be taken for granted if you don't feel the struggles. This is an excellent time to appreciate it all. This is where you find so much out about yourself. This is where you grow as a person. This is where you discover new adventures that open up your heart. This is where you take steps for a future that feels better for you and how you want to live. This is where you make decisions that build confidence and self-love. It is a great time to take in all the experience and not just hope it is over soon because it is too difficult. This is the part that makes it all worthwhile.

During your journey, you will discover new things and new firsts. Maybe your first massage, your first vacation, or your first outfit for a girls' day. Your first actual girls' day! You will find new things you enjoy doing and want to do. This will be a significant part of your journey. You don't want to miss this. You will have some worry, concern, fear, and confusion, but mostly joy, freedom, independence, courage, happiness, relief, and direction. That is a whole lot of greatness right there.

The most challenging times often lead to better days. They may be tough to get through, but they are stepping stones. Even your *nice girl* days (okay, years!) have been stepping stones to where you needed to be at those times. You may have met new friends and learned new interests, activities, or skills. It could have prepared you mentally for the challenges you will face with these changes. It could have shown you how much you want to focus on yourself and live your best life from here on out. Sometimes, you may see where things have led you; other times, it can feel like wasted time. Don't focus on wasted time. It's not wasted. Learn, grow, and find the positive. Sometimes, the positive can be hard to find. That is alright. It is still hidden in there somewhere.

The journey is such an important part to focus on. Again, this will not happen overnight, but gradually, it will all work together, and you will be in a much better place with yourself. You need to work on your goals daily, in any small way. It doesn't matter what you are working on. It must be watered to grow. If you go to school for a degree, you must take the classes, do the homework, stay up late, miss events to study, and usually do this for a few years. It is a process, a journey to work through before the degree. To start a business, you must find a location, figure out a business plan, get supplies, and get clients. Then, you will work hard to get the business into a financially solid place. If you want to lose weight, you need to make a plan for eating and exercising. You will have to wake up early, hit the gym (or your workout space), struggle with possibly hitting plateaus, and get frustrated, but still push on until it starts to take effect and you start seeing and feeling the results. The work is hard with any of these examples, but this is all you need to reach your destination. It will be no different here.

You may have struggles. You may feel that your energy is not being utilized effectively, or feel guilty that your energy is focused on you and not on others or things. This is normal. You have been focused on others for many years, possibly your entire life, and the change is very foreign and uncomfortable. This is a good thing. It means you are doing it and right where you need to be. Don't step back to get comfortable. You will find some misery there. Keep moving forward and face that uncomfortable feeling. As crazy as it may seem, this will be your happy place! This is where you are making change and knowing you are heading in the right direction. There may be an internal struggle, but that is okay. This is you growing, learning, adapting, and focusing on your needs and wants. This time can be challenging, but it is the best part of the journey.

You must take the path to get to the destination. The path could have detours. While on that path, you may also figure out that you want to change direction to a better destination. It's all about the journey. Embrace it!

Chapter Eleven

The Empowered Woman

At first, they will ask you why you are doing it ~
later they will ask you how you did it.

~Unknown

Look how far you have come. Isn't this exciting? You have been a *nice girl* for many years, while being a positive influence on many people. You have been rewarded in abundance for all the hard work you have accomplished. Whether it be making new friends, being a part of your kid's life, getting rewarded at your job, achieving things you didn't know you could, making many people happy with your excellent work, or just doing it because you wanted to, you did great! Now, putting this energy and these efforts towards yourself is even better.

How do you feel about making decisions for yourself? How do you feel about not being allowed to be used? How do you feel about not pounding yourself to the ground to get things done that you shouldn't have taken on in the first place? What do you think about having more free time? What do you think about doing what you have wanted for years but have been putting off?

This is still new and can be challenging. But it is fabulous! Being fully vested and willing to treat yourself with much-needed care and respect is wonderful. You will continue to make significant progress, which will get easier with time. The more you say 'yes' to what is good for you, the more you will continue to do it. The world will not fall apart. The motions in life will keep going. Some people may not be thrilled, but they will figure out how to do it without you. And let them. If you can advise them on how to do something, do that. But then move on and leave it in their hands.

Some people will notice your changes and be angry, especially if you have enabled them. They will not like that they have to think or do for themselves. You can be there for them if needed or in times of wanting to, but you can't always be the one to fix it. You need to let them fix what they need to. Just be there to provide support if they allow it. They may get upset to the point that they break ties with you. Let them. That would be their choice and isn't because of you. If they break that tie, do not let them make you feel bad for leaving them astray to do their work and projects, or make fundamental life decisions.

The enabled person can make you feel like you have let them down, but you let them down by not allowing them to live independently and make their own decisions. This can be anyone from a family member, friend, co-worker, or the PTA president. If you have been handling situations and taking on what someone else should, they may be upset that you are now thinking of yourself and not them. And they may make you feel bad about this. Guilty. You may desperately want to help them by not putting them in that situation, but don't. Do they feel bad for putting you in your situation or using you? Draining you? Pushing you? Hurting you? They need to find their own solutions, which do not include you fixing them. The more you are the *nice girl* in these situations, the more problems will continue. When you start saying 'yes' to yourself, the more you help them, too.

Some people will notice a change in you and have no idea what it is, but they will like it. They will see you in a different light. They will see *your* light. The glow you have around you. Many people put off a certain glow about them, and you will, too. Most people who are confident and happy with themselves shine. This isn't about high-power success confidence, but rather just a person who radiates goodness about them. People will see this in you because you are friendly, caring, and giving. But when you say no, it is because it just doesn't work for you; they understand that, and that is all it needs to be.

You will gain a certain amount of knowledge from people because of this. You will see your strength and confidence, not as a strong, complicated person, but as a centered one. Many people admire those who can make good decisions for themselves in a caring way. You will feel this way about yourself, too. How could you not be proud of yourself and admire your hard work in self-care and healing your mind and soul?

Sometimes, you give in and say yes to something you don't want to. You may beat yourself up for it and get upset and frustrated. You may feel like you let yourself down. Don't! Feel your emotions about that decision, brush them away, and move forward. It isn't taking you back; you did not fail, and you are still empowered. Be okay with your decisions, and keep moving on. Things happen in life. It isn't perfect, but you get back to it and stop focusing on that. These are learning experiences and remarkable moments to prepare you for the next time so that you don't make the same decision.

A considerable amount of information has brought you to this place. Some of the information you will relate to, and other information may not apply. But it is all helpful to understand that you no longer need to be in charge of five hundred events, two classrooms, the work award party, and your class reunion. That was an exaggeration, but it can be what life feels like for a *nice girl*. It's a great time just to be nice, take a load off, focus on what you want, and be yourself.

You are capable of making changes to better your life. You are the creator of your reality. You will sometimes do things you don't want to, which is okay. Do it and be done. You will sometimes fall short of your goals, but that is okay. Just pick right back up and continue on. It really can be just like this. You keep doing what you are doing and work at it until you are no longer working at it, and it is just a part of your life.

The guilt, anxieties, and fear of change continue to fade away. You feel better with each decision you make. Your confidence is getting stronger. Your health feels better mentally and physically. A weight is off your shoulders, and the turning in your gut subsides. And you live a wholesome life for yourself.

You have all the power to live a life based on your wants and needs. You have the courage to make these decisions and choices if you allow yourself to do so. All of this is your choice. All of this is the life you want to live. All of this is in your power because you are an empowered woman.

Empowerment: having the strength, confidence, and power to do things or make decisions for oneself. *You are her!*

Author's Message

"Time makes changes, and changes happen at the right time" ~ Toni Dowrey

I wrote this book with the intent of helping others. Although some information may seem repetitive, I have a plan for that. Many times, if we read something once, we don't remember; however, if we read it more than once or a few times, we are more likely to remember and take action. There are some key points that I want you to take in, feel, and believe.

I wrote this book because I have been a *nice girl* for as long as I can remember. All through school, early adulthood, and then in my late twenties and early thirties, life changed, and I did too. I stood up for myself in a few situations. Tough situations. Out-of-the-ordinary situations. It scared me, but at the same time, it felt freeing and beautiful. But then I went back to doing what I did best. I did what I thought others wanted, what would be good for my kids, what I needed to do for my job, and sank back into the *nice girl,* again.

I know other *nice girls.* All the ones I have spoken with don't want to be this way. I know I wanted to change. I know others need guidance and permission to change their behavior. I decided to write this book and share my thoughts. While there are some research references in the book, much of this is personal experience, knowledge, and opinion.

The problem was that this book took me years to write. It was a struggle, and I couldn't figure out why. Then, one day, it came to me. I was still the *nice girl.* The story wasn't finished, and I wasn't ready to finish the book. Many times, I would do something I didn't want to so I could please someone else and tell my mom about it. My mom would ask, "Aren't you writing about not doing that?" I would reply, "Yes, but I haven't finished reading the book yet." We would laugh, but knowing this needed to change was very frustrating. I was doing better, but not fully there.

Then, it came the way it should. I had been acting as a *nice girl* towards someone for a very long time. For almost twelve years, actually. This person was not pleasant behind my back, but to my face was as sweet as can be. I kept the peace by always being friendly and cordial, although I knew I wasn't being treated right out of her presence. Then, a situation happened that she was engaged in, and I was finally done. I was finished putting up with the nonsense. I went to a birthday party, and when she approached me in her expected way to hug me with all her fake sweetness, I did not get up to receive it. I told her I did not plan to communicate with her that day. I felt relief and freedom from her grip on me as she stood stunned and in awe. She has those grips on many, but I was set free at that moment. And still am to this day.

That was my life-changing moment. I was working on the process, but that day, the big fat YES to being true to myself started without guilt, shame, or resentment. I have continued to say YES to what works for me and NO to what doesn't. It hasn't always been easy, but I feel good about the decisions, knowing I am putting my best interest where it needs to be. I haven't lost friends or family if I say no to them because they understand. All those years of worry and pleasing others are gone. I now think it was a wasted worry, but not a waste of time, because I appreciate my 'yeses' and do not take any of them for granted.

I am not a doctor, psychologist, or health expert. This book is based on my own research and personal life experience. If you need professional assistance, please do seek it for yourself.

I wrote this book to help others not put off taking care of their well-being, not wait as long as I did, and to let them know it is alright to stop being the *nice girl*. After so many years, I've come to enjoy being a happy, *nice* person!

About the Author

Toni Dowrey is the author of "Finding You and Your Direction; 11 ways to find the real you. Toni is a Certified Life Coach and Motivational Speaker. She enjoys speaking and assisting others with their goals and dreams.

Toni grew up in the Pacific Northwest, where she enjoyed a range of activities and animals. After her children were grown, she and her husband spent four years in Virginia together. Although they loved their life in Virginia, they returned to the Pacific Northwest to be with their grandchildren and family.

Outside of writing, Toni enjoys creating art, making quilts, hiking, kayaking, gardening, and making crafts with her grandchildren.

www.ingramcontent.com/pod-product-compliance
Lightning Source LLC
Chambersburg PA
CBHW071452070426
42452CB00039B/1140